Sacred Numbers of Hinduism

Exploring Their Mysticism and Symbolism

JAYARAM V

First Edition

Published by
Pure Life Vision LLC
New Albany, Ohio

Sacred Numbers of Hinduism: Exploring Their Mysticism and Symbolism
Copyright © 2025 by Jayaram V. All rights reserved.
Published and Distributed Worldwide by Pure Life Vision LLC., USA.
First edition 2025

No part of this publication may be reproduced, stored in a retrieval system, or transmitted in any form or by any means, electronic, mechanical, photocopying, recording, scanning, or otherwise, now known or hereinafter invented, except for quotations in printed reviews, without the prior written, express permission of the publisher or the author. This strict copyright protection is meant to ensure the respect and integrity of the author's work. Requests to the publisher for permission to print portions of this book or for bulk purchase of the book should be addressed to Pure Life Vision LLC, PO Box 1003, 102 W Main St, New Albany, OH 43054.

NO AI TRAINING: Without in any way limiting the author's and publisher's exclusive rights under copyright, any use of this publication to "train" generative artificial intelligence (AI) technologies to generate text is expressly prohibited. The author reserves all rights to license uses of this work for generative AI training and development of machine learning language models.

Pure Life Vision LLC is a registered company in the U.S.A. Pure Life Vision books and E-Books are available through numerous bookstores, our websites, and our online store. For inquiries, please visit https://www.PureLifeVision.com.

Cover Design © Jayaram V

Library of Congress Publisher Cataloging-in-Publication Data

V, Jayaram, (Vemulapalli)
Sacred Numbers of Hinduism: Exploring Their Mysticism and Symbolism
p. cm
    LCCN: 2025935190
    ISBN-13: 978-1-935760-20-7
    ISBN-10: 1-935760-20-3

Cover Design by Jayaram V
Printed in the United States of America
10 9 8 7 6 5 4 3 2
First Edition 2025

Contents

Preface 11
Introduction 13
Zero, Shunya 22
One, Eka 29
Two, Dvi 35
Three, Triah 44
Four, Chatur 58
Five Panchan 69
Six, Shashtan 81
Seven Saptan 90
Eight, Ashtan 102
Nine, Navan 110
Ten, Dasan 118
Other Numbers 125
Numbers in Hindu Philosophy 137
Epilogue 147

About the Author

Jayaram V has authored over 3000 articles and 16 books, which include such notable works as Brahman, The Awakened Life, An Introduction to Hinduism, Bhagavadgita: Unveiling Gita's Secrets, Essays on the Bhagavadgita, Brahman, The Awakened Life, Hinduism, an Introduction, Selected Upanishads, Brihadaranyaka and Chandogya Upanishads, Shiva Sutras: Mystic Knowledge Explained, The Hindu Caste System, etc. His writings are appreciated all over the world for their originality and quality of information and his analysis and interpretation of ancient texts. Jayaram V has studied Hinduism and related religions for over 40 years and writes regularly about various aspects of Hinduism, Buddhism, Jainism, spirituality, yoga, and self-improvement. Through his writings, he brings out the knowledge found in the ancient texts, their hidden symbolism, and the significance of various key concepts found in them and interprets them objectively with modern insights and without sectarian biases. His scientific and spiritual background helps him examine the subjects analytically with an open mind and maintain objectivity in his writings and interpretations. He combines the mundane and finite aspects of life with the mystical and transcendental without losing sight of their spiritual and practical value in today's world. Inspired by Swami Vivekananda, Sri Aurobindo, and several other spiritual masters of the past and present, he founded Hinduwebsite.com in 2000 to counter negative propaganda and share authentic information about Hinduism and related religions. He believes in religious tolerance and the fundamental freedom of everyone to choose their faith or belief system according to their nature, needs, and preferences. He believes that atheism is also a part of one's spiritual journey. His efforts have helped make ancient Hindu texts more accessible to the world audience and appreciate the teachings found in them. His work has helped bring the wisdom of India's oldest religious and spiritual traditions to people around the world and educate and inspire them. You can explore more of his writings on Jayaramv.com and Hinduwebsite.com.

Books By Jayaram V

The Bhagavadgita: Unveiling the Gita's Secrets, 2024

Shiva Sutras: Mystic Knowledge Explained, 2024

The Awakened Life: Spiritual Knowledge from India's Sacred Traditions, 2024

Brihadaranyaka Upanishad, Revised 2024

Chandogya Upanishad, Revised 2024

The Bhagavadgita: A Simple Translation, Second Edition, 2024

Introduction to Hinduism, Second Edition, 2024

Brahman, Second Edition, 2025

Bhagavadgita, Main Teachings and Concepts, 2025

The Hindu Caste System, 2025

Sacred Numbers of Hinduism, 2025

The Bhagavadgita: A Complete Translation

Selected Upanishads

Think Success: Essays on Self-help

Being the Best: Practical Advice for Peace and Happiness

Thoughts and Quotations

Sadhana Panchakam - The Fivefold Spiritual Practice

Preface

This book elaborates on an article I wrote several years ago about the symbolic significance of numbers in Hinduism. It was based on my knowledge of Hinduism and my intuitive awareness of how the numbers correlated with various beliefs and practices associated with the faith. The article was well received. The idea itself came to me after I read Socrates's work on the mystic significance of numbers. I started thinking about zero, and soon I realized that zero perfectly symbolized Brahman and His indeterminate state. It is definitely the starting point of all numbers, and just as everything is said to dissolve into Brahman at the end of creation, all numbers dissolve into zero through multiplication. From there, I thought of other numbers and their symbolic significance presented itself to me. The essay I wrote was very long. In fact, I had to cut down a lot of information since it was meant for the Internet. However, I decided at that time that I should write a book about it in the future. It took several years to complete that sankalpa.

In this book, I aimed to present in some detail many aspects of the hidden symbolism and religious importance associated with each of the basic numbers from one to nine and other numbers in popular usage. The book has fourteen chapters, excluding the preface and epilogue. In the introduction, I explained how ancient Indians used numbers to organize their knowledge about creation and the order of divinities. The second chapter addresses the concept of zero, its universal symbolism of emptiness, nothingness, and immeasurability. It outlines the historical development of zero in India and its significance in Hinduism as a symbol of infinity and the Nirguna Brahman, the Unmanifested Brahman. Chapters three to eleven explore the multiple meanings of numbers from one to nine, their meanings according to gender and case, their uniqueness and symbolism, and what they represent in Hindu cosmology, God's manifestations, the Hindu pantheon, and various other aspects of creation.

Chapter 12 presents the symbolic significance of the number ten. Although it is not a base number, it occupies an important place in the historical development of the decimal system. Hinduism recognizes its religious and spiritual symbolism, suggesting how it represents wholeness, completeness, dualities, the harmony of the opposites, perfection, all-encompassing reality, mortal life, diversity, and more. In the next chapter, you will find information on numbers higher than ten, their symbolic meanings, and associations with various concepts and divinities. At the end, I added a new chapter on the numbers in Hindu philosophy.

Most of the interpretations in this book are either my own or gleaned from various sources. While presenting them, I may have become overenthusiastic in unravelling the hidden connections and symbolism associated with the numbers. The central purpose of this effort is to draw your attention to the fact that numbers are hidden and at work in various objects, structures, and functions of our existence, including our bodies and the world or universe in which we live. If you understand that and if it can ignite your curiosity to explore the subject further, I believe the purpose is well served.

Jayaram V
05/07/2025

Introduction

"The ingenious method of expressing every possible number using a set of ten symbols (each symbol having a place value and an absolute value) emerged in India. The idea seems so simple nowadays that its significance and profound importance is no longer appreciated. Its simplicity lies in the way it facilitated calculation and placed arithmetic foremost amongst useful inventions." Laplace, a French mathematician.

Each of us has had our early encounters with numbers. In those formative years of early learning, we form a definitive opinion about whether we are comfortable with numbers and mathematical computations or find our comfort and ease in other subjects where we excel and feel good, or make our mark. I do not remember exactly when I learned to count. However, I vaguely remember my mother teaching me how to count basic numbers and memorize multiplication tables. Before I went to school and built upon that early knowledge and learning, I could see whether having more of something I liked was better than having less, what circumstances favored me, or worked to my advantage when I competed with my sister or others for something. I knew I was better off than the tribal kids who played in the street in front of the government bungalow with a spacious compound and large trees where we lived. Their mothers worked hard in the huts that stood a little distance away under a canopy of large trees on the other side of the street, pounding rice rhythmically with wooden pestles to separate the husk from the grain. They seemed happy as they pounded the rice, singing tribal songs in chorus as if they were part of a musical show. They were illiterate but knew how much rice they needed for the day and whether they had pounded enough grain. They also knew how to quote or haggle as they bargained for the right prices at the weekly fair held in the village and bought or sold items such as honey, fruit, milk, grains, or vegetables.

Reminiscing about those days in retrospect, I can say that humanity does not require a deeper knowledge of mathematics to survive.

They can survive even if they do not know how to count or calculate. However, although people can technically live without a formal knowledge of mathematics, and can manage with their instincts, experience, and observation, it is doubtful how much progress they can achieve or how precisely they think, build their wealth or lives or solve their problems. Indeed, some cultures and languages are found to be "anumeric" or "numberless, which means they lack names for specific numbers beyond two or three. For example, the Pirahã people of the Amazon [1] rainforest do not have words for exact numbers in their spoken language, only general terms for quantities like "few" or "many." Similarly, some indigenous groups in Australia and South America have a limited numerical vocabulary, often ending at three. However, further studies showed that people belonging to these "numberless" groups had an innate ability to learn higher numbers when they were taught.

At one time, India (and several other nations) had a literacy rate of about 20%, which meant that approximately 80% of the population could not write, read, or count. Yet, the country survived and emerged as one of the economic powerhouses of the world as the literacy rate improved and people could harness their higher cognitive functions with improved brain power, neural efficiency, and math training. We have an innate ability to manage our lives and circumstances with whatever resources are available to us. Even the earliest human communities managed to cultivate lands, raise crops, rear cattle, store surplus grain, and barter food and other items amidst floods and natural calamities. They relied on ingenious methods to keep track of their possessions, the animals they hunted or domesticated, the wealth they acquired, the number of their children, grandchildren, and relations, and the land their tribes controlled. If they were drawn into conflicts and skirmishes with other groups, they knew who was missing. They also kept track of the distances they travelled to gather food, explore their surroundings, or find suitable habitats for hunting, fishing, or building new settlements. However, compared to the present-day world, they belonged to a primitive world where people could thrive with limited knowledge, education, and numerical ability.

Numbers play both positive and negative roles in our lives.

Historically, they have significantly contributed to the development of human civilization. Advances in the fields of mathematics and science have led to substantial improvements in our knowledge of engineering, architecture, urban development, trade, commerce, economics, accounting, timekeeping, digital and space technology, computing, artificial intelligence, communication, navigation, and many other fields. In our lives, numbers help us excel, overachieve, stay ahead in competition, earn more, win battles, and test our strength, skills, superiority, or progress in life.

Numbers shaped my early life. In elementary school, when I took my first exam and scored the highest marks in the class, my grandfather responded positively, saying he was proud of my achievement, but cautioned me not to take it for granted or feel too comfortable. He said that I must keep working hard to stay ahead of others in the class. Hard work, discipline, and dedication would lead me on the road to success. His words made me feel happy, motivated me, and strengthened my resolve to excel in my studies. I kept working hard, following a rigorous routine, without anyone telling me. As a result, I always stood first or second in the class and earned the respect of my teachers and elders. Thus, numbers helped me exceed my expectations, year after year, and forge ahead in my life, overcoming my doubts and limitations.

However, numbers can also complicate our lives. At times, they can make us feel inferior, outsmarted, defeated, envious, and miserable when we fail to reach our goals and meet our expectations. They can also negatively impact our thoughts and actions, strengthening our egos, inciting our desires and passions, and making us feel selfish and self-centered. They influence group behavior and the social dynamics of human populations. They can set trends, cause friction among people, create class distinctions, social hierarchies, group conflicts, economic and social disparities, and trade imbalances. This may lead to anger, alienation, discrimination, groupthink, wars, civil wars, poverty, crime, violence, and suffering. Our increased knowledge and excessive reliance on numbers in the development of our civilization have also led to many problems. For example, they have resulted in disparities between the rich and poor, social injustices, mass migrations, social upheavals, fraud, and corruption, as statistical comparisons largely guide our value system and create various imbalances along with social and economic inequities. Therefore, we can say that while the world has greatly benefited from our knowledge of numbers and mathematics, it has also created widespread human suffering and insurmountable problems.

Numbers are hidden in every aspect of our existence, including our religious and spiritual lives. They carry a great cultural and religious significance, not only in Hinduism or any scripture, but across all religions and spiritual philosophies. Pythagoras (570 BCE- 475 BCE) is believed to be the first notable philosopher and teacher who proposed that numbers contain hidden symbolism and cryptic messages. He suggested that the principles governing numbers not only determine all existential realities found in the world but are also derived from them or their permutations and combinations. However, many scholars believe that Pythagoras was not the first philosopher to perceive the hidden symbolism or spiritual significance of numbers. He probably derived his ideas from other teachers and masters since, in his early life, he visited Egypt, Syria, and India and assimilated the knowledge of several ancient cultures. After exploring the mystical practices in these ancient lands, he returned to Greece and established a school or university in Crotona, a Dorian colony in Southern Italy. He believed that the number symbols pointed to virtues in general and that each number was related to one or more of them. Therefore, by contemplating the numbers, one could strengthen those virtues or develop desired qualities and potencies.

With developments in science and technology, we know that numbers serve as basic raw materials or building blocks in the structure and function of the material universe as well as in the workings of Nature and her myriad forces. They are evident in the configuration and energy fields of atoms and quanta, and classical as well as quantum mechanics. Hence, understanding and unravelling the mysteries of the universe and the functioning of Nature is greatly facilitated through mathematics. Indeed, much of the progress we have achieved in the last two centuries can be attributed to our knowledge of mathematics, which has also improved our understanding in other areas, including physics, chemistry, biology, and industrial technology. Without even realizing it, we instinctively use numbers every day when we operate machines, use gadgets, drive a vehicle, navigate through a crowded area, draw plans, work on projects, or set goals.

Numbers are ingrained in our awareness and spatial perception. When we hear a sound, our mind can guess from which direction it may be coming and how far away it is. Without consciously calculating, we can determine the distance we should maintain to feel safe from other things and people or safeguard ourselves. This knowledge has given us an edge in our struggle for survival on the planet and has greatly contributed to our success as a species and the success of our civilization. However, at the same time, it is also true that numbers do not preexist in our consciousness. We must learn them through study or observation, just like any other knowledge about any subject. We are also not good at calculating time, heights, or distances without external aids. Some people possess an extraordinary ability to make huge calculations mentally, some can do it with effort or training, while some cannot even do simple calculations with ease. We still do not know whether genetic differences are responsible for this or if other factors contribute to it. These observations clearly establish that numbers do not preexist in our consciousness and that we must learn them consciously until they are firmly implanted in our minds, just like any other knowledge.

Much of our knowledge of numbers is based on assumptions. For example, the argument that the difference between one and two or two and three is one is assumed based on physical counting, calculations, and the relative values of each number. However, since numbers do not have an absolute or physical existence, except in our minds, this cannot be proven definitively. The conclusion that any number, no matter how large, when multiplied by zero, results in zero is also an assumption because zero does not exist in reality except as a concept or as the absence or nonexistence of something. Furthermore, we presume that the basic numbers from 1 to 9 are universal constants, meaning their values are stable and permanent in all situations. However, this may change in the future with further progress in quantum mechanics, where everything seems fluid and indeterminate. For example, if multiple universes or realities exist, as quantum mechanics suggests, how does each number exist in a multiverse? Will their values remain constant in all the universes or vary? Another interesting facet of numbers is that although they seem to validate many aspects of our experiential reality in mathematical computations, equations, and operations, there is no physical evidence that each of them exists physically in the universe in any observable form or condition. In this regard, they are closer to God since neither of their existence can be proven independently and with certainty. The notion of infinity is also an assumption from a purely rational perspective since there is no observable infinite reality that can be proven or established materially.

Whatever the truth may be, in today's world, it isn't easy to survive without a basic knowledge of elementary mathematics and simple numerical operations. Whether we are managing money or investments, cooking, managing time, planning an event or budget, traveling, navigating, shopping, performing simple to complex technical jobs, engaging in construction, logical thinking, problem solving, negotiating deals, or writing an exam, we depend on numbers to manage our lives and improve our circumstances - sometimes without even noticing it. In the history of civilization, perhaps the invention of numbers was as important as the invention of language, fire, and tools such as the wheel.

Although much of what happens around us or in this universe seems random, one can see the play of numbers and several mathematical principles even in the random processes. Indian seers and sages recognized this play of numbers in our lives and destinies three or four millenniums ago. They experimented with various number systems before inventing the decimal system sometime during the Gupta or Pre-Gupta period. Numbers are mentioned in all the ancient texts of Hinduism, including the Vedas. Those who studied the Vedas and practiced Vedism believed in the concept of Rta (Rita), the universal rhythm, which manifested in the recurring and repetitive patterns of days, nights, months, lunar and solar cycles, seasons, and so on. They believed that numbers were hidden in those recurring patterns and in the forces that caused them with mathematical precision, and associated numbers with them.

They also noticed similar patterns in human life and attributed the

Rta that manifested them to the power of Brahman. They divided human life into four phases and prescribed different duties for each phase, in addition to dividing humanity into four classes and assigning different duties and obligations for each. They perceived Brahman as Eka (the One), Prathama, the First, and Adi (before all); life as characterized by dualities; creation as having three primary functions (creation, preservation, and destruction); space as divided into four quarters; and physical nature as consisting of five elements and six seasons, among others. They recognized Time as a divine force that was both auspicious and inauspicious, as well as constructive and destructive, exerting positive and negative influence upon people according to their karma. As a destructive force, it was Death itself that sealed the fate of everyone in the mortal world. Therefore, they placed great importance on calculating an auspicious place and time before undertaking any important religious or secular work.

The well-planned and well-developed Indus Valley cities with streets intersecting each other at right angles, neatly laid out structures, and an advanced and efficient drainage system reveal that their inhabitants possessed a sound knowledge of mathematics and geometric patterns. As traders and seafarers, they developed navigation and used precise weights and measures for trading and traveling to distant lands. The tablets found in the excavations show that they also kept a record of their activities and probably used number forms for commercial transactions.

Even in subsequent periods, Indians relied on their knowledge of numbers and computational skills to construct complex sacrificial altars, religious monuments such as stupas, royal palaces, moats, fortifications, and temples. They also used these skills to sculpt stone and wooden images of gods and goddesses with precision, measure distances, charge taxes, calculate time, determine and forecast auspicious moments and celestial events, observe and record the movement of stars and planets, and commemorate important events such as the start of an era or the birth of an important person. At some point, they also began using the decimal system, which was subsequently adopted by other cultures and the whole world.

In ancient India, people led very religious lives. They prayed and worshipped several divinities in whom they had faith. They believed that the purpose of human life was to achieve liberation from the cycle of births and deaths and ascend to sunlit worlds. They did not believe in withdrawing from life or abnegating duty as a necessary condition to pursue God. Enjoyment of life and material wealth were important goals of human life, but not the ultimate. The highest aim was moksha or liberation from the delusions and distractions of life through spiritual discipline and self-surrender. The best way to achieve it was through a divine-centered life, where every activity was meant to achieve inner purity and experience God as the witness, guardian, guide, and rescuer.

They reflected this attitude in many aspects of their lives. Whether in their professional or vocational duties, the study of the Vedas, tending to the cattle, or engaging in some mundane affairs, they sought the intervention of divinities through the practice of dharma. They reflected the same attitude towards numbers, believing them to be symbols of transcendental realities or truths, each having its own potency and symbolic significance. They thought the numbers could be useful for practicing religious or spiritual disciplines or contemplating the divinities and their attributes to stabilize their minds and envision them directly in higher states of self-absorption. Indeed, they used number names to designate each day in the fortnight of the lunar calendar, determine the number of divinities in each group receiving offerings during the sacrifices, or estimate their relative importance in the pantheon or in assisting humanity.

To the intuitive seekers of Brahman, who retired to forests and secluded places to practice penance in search of liberation and freedom from birth and death, like the ascetics idolized in the Mundaka Upanishad, numbers presented many opportunities to meditate upon and realize their hidden symbolism. In the following chapters, we will explore the symbolic significance hidden in the numbers from zero to ten. In doing so, we will also realize why the decimal system and the use of present-day symbols for numbers originated in ancient India.

References

1. Everett, Caleb, Linguistic relativity and numeric cognition: New light on a prominent test case, University of Miami

Zero, Shunya

I do not recall when and how I learned about zero. I believe I became aware of it when I learned other numbers and basic math. Zero became an integral part of our lives when we began taking class tests in the elementary school I attended. Whenever someone scored a zero on a test, it became the event of the day, inviting laughter and ridicule from teachers and students alike. It was like the headline news of the day. The fact that someone fared worse than everyone else in the test amused the class, except the victims who had to endure the ignominy for a few days both in the class and at home. Teachers would make examples of the laggards in the class by giving them harsh punishments or extra homework. If the news reached their parents, they received punishments from them too. Therefore, students wanted to avoid the humiliation of scoring zero by all means, or being laughed at, especially by the girls in the class. From an early age, we were thus conditioned to accept zero as a symbol of failure and humiliation, which made no one happy. Zero is the first number among the basic digits, but in our value system, it has no value unless it is associated with other numbers. 10 is always better than one, and 100 is even better.

Zero has that special status. It evokes different emotions in different people, depending on the circumstances. Although it does not have a numerical value, in almost all languages and across all cultures, it is a universal symbol of emptiness, nothingness, worthlessness, failure, or lack of something that we want or cherish. Who wants to be a zero in life? Yet, by becoming a zero only, a yogi or an ascetic achieves liberation. Zero signifies nothing in material life, but is the cherished goal of the monks and yogis in spiritual life. For them, emptiness is the state of having nothing, owning nothing, desiring nothing, and not worrying about anything. One becomes a zero through renunciation by giving up everything: past, present, name, family, possessions, relationships, and even religion. We thus have a strange relationship with zero. No one wants a zero or desires to be a zero, but most people wish to add zeros to their wealth or bank balances. Those zeros enhance your status and image in society and bring you name and fame.

Zero is a universal symbol. No one needs to explain what it means. It has the same mathematical notation (0) in all languages, and everyone can recognize it when they see it. It also conveys different meanings in different contexts. In English, it can be used as a noun, verb, or adjective to suggest different meanings. For example, you zero in on a solution or cause when you understand a problem or situation, or when you know exactly what happened. We may have zero influence over what happens or does not happen, especially if the situation is beyond our control. Ground zero refers to the epicenter, or a place where a violent and destructive event, catastrophe, or calamity happens. Companies that record zero growth year after year are bound to fail. No one wants to be a zero in life or take credit for zero achievement or for something that has zero value, utility, or significance. All journeys and movements begin from a starting point called the zero-point. In a zero-sum game, the net outcome is zero since the losses equal the wins. If two parties are involved, the gains of one party equal the losses of the other party. Although zero is frequently used today in many instances, according to the Merriam-Webster Dictionary, it is said to have been first used in English in 1598. Before that, probably naught was used to mean zero or nothingness. In some literary expressions, the word cipher is also used instead of zero since it has the same etymological root, the Arabic *sifr*.

A brief history of zero

The concept of zero as something of no value likely prevailed in almost all ancient cultures. Anyone who bartered goods knew that when they exchanged equal-value items, they owed nothing to each other. However, most people in those cultures did not know how to express it in writing. Sumerian scribes used empty spaces to denote zero or the absence of numbers or value about 4000 years ago. Babylonians (300 BCE) used empty spaces to convey zeros in their sexagesimal, or base 60, system to distinguish between numbers of different magnitudes (such as 10, 100, or 1000). However, neither of them used zero as a numeral or a number in itself. In other words, in both these systems, it was cumbersome and confusing to distinguish numbers that were in multiples of tens, hundreds, or thousands.

Neither the Egyptians, the Greeks, nor the Romans had any use for zero since their number system was not based on place values but symbols. Since each number had to be marked separately, it was a cumbersome system that limited the use of numbers with large values. The Mayans (350 CE) in South America developed an entirely independent place-value number system based on 20 to measure time, in which they used different symbols to denote zeros in their calendars. None of these systems considered it worthwhile to use a number form or symbol to mark zeros in their numeral or mathematical calculations or to express fractional values.

That remarkable development happened in India, where the decimal system evolved independently. Indians likely used zero for a long time as a number to represent nil values or in the decimal system to represent fractions. However, literary evidence of this is found only in a seventh-century work known as *Brahmasphuta Siddhanta* (628 CE) by an Indian mathematician, Brahmagupta. He not only expressed zero as a number but also used it in calculations such as additions and subtractions. It is very likely that he did not invent zero but adapted an existing system. Indian philosophers, astrologers, seers, and sages used numbers profusely in their calculations to measure time, determine auspicious times, measure the lengths of bricks to build sacrificial altars, or design them in different geometrical formations. They likely used them in other matters also, such as sculpting images, building temples and other structures, paying dues and wages, charging interest or taxes, or conducting trade and commerce. Besides its numerical significance, zero also symbolizes emptiness (shunya). Hence, it has great significance in the metaphysical doctrines of both Hinduism and Buddhism. Thus, in recorded history, zero gained prominence as a placeholder and a number for the first time in India. It also set in motion remarkable developments in the field of mathematics, expanding its scope and facilitating complex computations.

Subsequently, the use of zero spread from India to places like Cambodia in the Far East and China. Historians traced a seventh-century inscription in the ruins of a Hindu temple in Cambodia in which zero was used to mark the year 605 of the Saka era in Khmer numerals. Persian and Arab scholars who translated the Indian works introduced zero to the Islamic world in the eighth century CE, resulting in significant advancements in science and mathematics in the Arab world. Muslim scholars not only extended the use of zero in algebra, arithmetic, and geometry as a placeholder and a numeral but also introduced it to Europe.

Zero in Hinduism

Although India is the birthplace of zero, strangely, there is no specific word for it in Sanskrit. Before the numerals were introduced, it was represented as 'kha,' which means a hole, empty space, or shunya, a generic and philosophical term that has multiple meanings, such as empty, void, nothing, vacant, absent, non-existent, etc. Later, it was represented as Zero '0'. In Hindu philosophy, shunya does not mean emptiness or void but the absence or nonexistence of something. It also refers to an indeterminate state from which creation manifests. A thing may become nonexistent for various reasons – when it is moved to another place, altered, replaced by something else, hidden from view, or destroyed. In Buddhism, emptiness has different philosophical connotations. It may mean the absence of something or an absolute and indescribable state in which all perceptions, ego-sense, duality, becoming and being, awareness, otherness, etc., disappear, and the mind rests in itself. We will discuss these differences later.

In Hinduism, zero is not only a numeral with cosmic significance but also a mystic symbol. Just as the number eight, which is often used to symbolize infinity, zero also represents infinity, the never-ending cycles of creation, preservation, and destruction progressing through an endless loop. It also serves as a symbolic or numerical representation of the Nirguna Brahman, also known as the Unmanifested Brahman, who is eternal, indestructible, absolute, unchangeable, and without qualities, names, and forms. Indeed, the shunyam in Sanskrit also means Brahman, the eternal mystery. Very little is known about him. He is the known unknown.

So is zero. No one knows for sure what this number is, what it represents, and what its true value is. All that we know about it are merely assumptions. The physical laws of the universe do not apply to zero. It stands as a bridge between the physical and the metaphysical realms and between reason and faith. It is indefinable and can be explained only in terms of "not this" and "not that." It is indivisible, without form, without qualities, without a beginning, and without an end. It is difficult to say whether it exists or not, whether it is a number or not, because no one knows for sure.

The Bhagavadgita (8.18) declares, *"From the Unmanifested, all the manifested things come into existence at the dawn of the Day. At the approach of Night, they all dissolve in That only, which is known as the Unmanifested."* Indeed, Brahman is the eternal constant, the zero. He neither manifests nor unmanifests. What manifests or unmanifests in creation, or what comes into existence, is Prakriti (Nature), which is an integral and inseparable aspect of Him. In Her unmanifested (asambhuta) aspect, She is the Primal Prakriti or Mula Prakriti, the root of all. In Her manifested (sambhuta), she represents the energy, materiality, and source of all creation. This combination of Brahman and His energy or materiality is described in the scriptures as Purusha and Prakriti or Shiva and Shakti. Their union is depicted symbolically in the imagery as Shivalingam and worshipped by devotees in numerous Shiva and Shakti temples all over the world. In the mystic diagrams (yantras and mandalas) used in Tantric rituals and meditative practices of Hindus and Buddhists, their union is depicted as Bindu, the dot, or the eternal zero. The dot is placed at the center of the tantric diagrams and mandalas to denote that it is the source of all and that everything manifests from it. Everything arises from it, and everything eventually dissolves in it. It is the only constant in the whole existence.

For Buddhists, that dot represents emptiness as well as Nirvana. For Hindus, it represents the unmanifested Brahman (asambhuta). He is the ultimate and absolute source of all. From Him arises the whole creation: all the numbers, letters, sounds, words, languages, names, forms, worlds, beings, states, conditions, birth, death, samsara, suffering, bondage, liberation, in short, all existence. Seated in Prakriti as the Self of all, He enjoys His play of creation. Hindu schools of philosophy do not believe that existence sprang out of nothing. For every effect, there must be a cause. Effects manifest by the transformation, separation, projection, expression, or concealment of their causes. Similarly, nonexistence (Asat) does not mean emptiness but the absence of material existence (Sat) or the diversity of names and forms. By this analogy, the zero is not emptiness but represents the null value or the absence of a specific value or number. In ancient India, numbers had no specific symbols (1,2, etc.). They followed an alphasyllabic numeral system in which each letter in the Sanskrit alphabet carried a value. At least three numeral systems were in use: the Aryabhaṭa, Katapayadi, and the Aksharapalli numeral systems. For example, in the Aryabhata system, the constants (Vargas) from Ka to Ma in the Sanskrit alphabet were assigned numbers 1, 2,3, and up to 25. The letters (avargas) from Ya to Ha were assigned 30, 40, 50, and up to 100. The vowels A to Ha were assigned exponents of 100, like 1, 100, 10^4, 10^6, and so on.

No wonder that, because of this, the entire Sanskrit alphabet is considered in Hinduism as a number table or the wheel of the Mother (Matrka Chakra). Each number is a matra, which has multiple meanings: number, measure of unity, a letter, moment or a unit of time, a music note, particle, atom, wealth, matter, the material world, and so on. Thus, if zero represents Asambhuta, the unmanifested and indeterminate Brahman, all the numbers, letters, the material world, and the whole creation represent Sambhuta, the manifested creation made possible by the union of Purusha and Prakriti.

Thus, in Hinduism, zero is not merely emptiness or nothingness (shunya) but an indeterminate state from which all numbers (causes and effects) manifest and into which all numbers are finally resolved. It is the Aum of all numbers or the starting and ending point (bindu) of all the numbers one can imagine. Probably for this reason, the scholars of ancient India initially used a dot to mark the zero in their writings and inscriptions. To depict the numbers, they used the Sanskrit alphabet.

Still, zero is a mystery. Because of its indeterminate nature, it defies logic and can jeopardize the integrity of any mathematical equation or calculation. Maybe it is the boundary between matter and antimatter or between existence and nonexistence. Maybe it is the void where nothing exists except itself as the starting point of all possibilities and probabilities. Finite and infinite, the first and the last, the smallest and so also the largest of all, it could neither be destroyed nor created. It is an eternal constant, the Bindu, the small atom or matra, that will survive and remain immutable even if the whole universe is dissolved or when Isvara, the Universal Lord of Creation, goes into a deep sleep at the end of each cycle of creation. In creation, you can find it everywhere, hidden in every number and aspect of creation. Any number, when it collides with zero, as in multiplication, becomes zero, just as any inimical force that collides with Isvara is instantly destroyed. However, when placed correctly or in the right order among other numbers, it multiplies or increases their values. For example, when placed before a number, it does not add any value, but when placed after it, its value is multiplied by ten. Zero is thus a very apt symbol of the Supreme Brahman. No other symbol in our knowledge can represent Him, His absolute state, perfection, and completeness, with such clarity and simplicity. The significance of Brahman is symbolically summed up in the following Sanskrit verse found in the Brihadaranyaka Upanishad (5.1). It can equally be applied to zero.

Aum, puranam adah, purnam idam, purnat purnam udacyate purnasya purnam adaya purnam evavasisyate. aum kham brahma, kham puranam, vayuram kham, iti ha smahakauravyayani-putrah, vedo'yam brahmana viduh; ve dainenayad veditavyam. iti prathamam brahmanam.

Aum! That is full. This is full. From the full arises the full. Even after taking the full off the full, the full still remains full. Thus, verily, the sons of Kauravyayani used to say, "Aum is spatial Brahman, space that is ancient, space that is filled with air." This is the knowledge that the knower of Brahman knows. Through it, one knows what is to be known.

One, Eka

One of the oddities of the Sanskrit language is that words and numbers have grammatical cases, numbers, and gender forms. In other words, their base forms and pronunciations may change for each grammatical case (bhakti), number (vachana), and gender (linga). Unlike English, Sanskrit has three grammatical numbers: singular, dual, and plural, three genders: masculine (pullingam), feminine (strilingam), and neuter (napumsaka lingam), and seven grammatical cases (vibhakti) instead of three. The basic form of a word or number may change according to any of these criteria. For example, the following table shows how the base form of number one (eka) changes according to the three genders and seven cases.

Case	Masculine	Feminine	Neuter
Nominative (Prathama)	Ekā	Ekā	Ekam
Accusative (Dvitiya)	Ekām	Ekām	Ekam
Instrumental (Tritiya)	Ekena	Ekayā	Ekena
Dative (Chaturthi)	Ekasmai	Ekasyai	Ekasmai
Ablative (Panchami)	Ekasmat	Ekasyāḥ	Ekasmat
Genitive (Shashti)	Ekasya	Ekasyāḥ	Ekasya
Locative (Saptami)	Ekasmin	Ekasyām	Ekasmin

In Sanskrit, eka has multiple meanings: one, single, alone, only, not accompanied by anyone, the same, firm, unchanged, unique, chief, supreme, peerless, etc. In English, we can also use one differently in different contexts. However, such variations are comparatively limited. In worldly life, one denotes supreme and unparalleled power, position, status, sovereignty, uniqueness, and aloneness. One is a universal symbol of unity, primacy, independence, self-existence, and distinction. According to the school of Pythagoras, it is the first odd number that, when added to an odd number, results in an even number, and when added to an even number, results in an odd number. Hence, it is called an "evenly odd" number 1. Pythagoreans, Greek philosophers such as Aristotle who followed him, and theosophists called it the Monad. They equated it with God, the first of everything, the Creator, intelligence, the void, the sun, and many other things.

Theon of Smyrna, a Pythagorean philosopher, considered it a stable, firm, immutable, and indivisible number, since when multiplied by itself, it remains unchanged, and when any other number is multiplied by it, that number also remains unchanged. In numerology, the number one is regarded as the starting point—the first step in a journey, representing independence, originality, and initiation. Hence, New Year's Day is celebrated on January 1st. It is also considered to symbolize the sun or God Himself, who is symbolically worshipped as the sun in many cultures since ancient times. In many cultures, the number also symbolizes the whole creation when viewed as a single entity emerging from God or a supernatural power. Proclus, a Greek Neoplatonist philosopher, equated it with the world itself.

In Hinduism, Brahman as Isvara, the Lord of the Universe, is considered the one and only. In creation, the One becomes many. One can also convey distinction as in "one of the best" or "one of the foremost." Ganesha is known as Ekadanta since he has only one tusk. Ekantam means aloneness, solitariness, exclusiveness, or an absolute and indivisible state. Ekaaksharam means Aum since it is a monosyllable. Ekagrata means unwavering concentration or attention. In devotional worship, serving only one deity exclusively is known as ekantaseva or ekantatva. A sovereign with unrivaled power and control is known as ekachakradhipati. The word Prathama also represents the number one. It means, first and foremost, the earliest, the most ancient, first in line of succession, primeval, and primary. A king is the first among his subjects, just as the president of a nation is. In Hinduism, the firstborn son has certain rights and privileges. God is Prathama because He is before all.

Number one is a symbolic representation of God, Isvara, Saguna Brahman, or Brahman with qualities and forms. All the meanings of eka mentioned above perfectly fit the attributes of Brahman and His manifestations, especially that of Purusha, Isvara, the Cosmic Being, or the Lord of the Universe. Isvara is the First Born, the Cosmic Being, God, or Brahman, with materiality and awakened Prakriti (sambhuta). In the Vedas, He is often called Brahma, the creator. With the help of Prakriti, He projects the worlds and the entire creation, containing within Himself all that He manifests. He is the Lord and Controller of all, the Supreme Universal Being and the Highest Deity of the Bhagavadgita, Vedas, and Tantras, who is also known by several other names such as Sada Shiva, Parameswara, Narayana, Jagannatha, Para Brahma, the Cosmic Self, Hiranyagarbha, Viraj, Purusha, Adi Purusha, etc. As the Lord of the Universe, He creates the worlds and beings with His Shaktis (powers) and inviolable will.

Brahma, Vishnu, Shiva, who represent the Trinity, and the rest of the gods and goddesses are His functional aspects. They uphold and ensure the order and regularity of all creation by performing their respective obligatory duties (dharmas). He rescues those who perform their obligatory duties selflessly and uphold righteousness (Dharma) or those who surrender to Him and spend their lives in His contemplation and devotion, renouncing desires. The Kena Upanishad (4.6) states that He should be worshipped as tadvanam, meaning the reality which is the abode and source of all and which is fit for worship, adoration, or contemplation. The scriptures also declare that He is eternal, indescribable, indestructible, and beyond the grasp of the mind and senses, bliss consciousness, and is known and experienced by yogis in the transcendental state of oneness or self-absorption (samadhi) only. By knowing him, everything is known. By realizing Him, one reaches the end of samsara, duality, division, delusion, and suffering. In creation, He becomes many.

Thus, the One (eka) becomes aneka (many) due to the divisions and multiplications of Prakriti's aspects. Oneness (ekatvam) or aloneness (kaivalya) is also the goal of the yogis. By attaining oneness or experiential unity (ekarasa) through concentration (ekagrata) and exclusive devotion (ekabhakti), they enter the absolute and indistinguishable state (zero) of Brahman. In Tantra, zero (Bindu) represents the unmanifested Brahman. In creation, He becomes Purusha, the One, containing within Himself Prakriti, His dynamic force and materiality, in her awakened or manifested mode (sambhuta). Their union results in the formation of jivas, each containing both. In each jiva, Prakriti represents the body and its parts, while Purusha represents the Self. Of all the jivas, humans are the perfect examples of their union.

Hence, the Vedas describe a human being as a miniature Isvara, each containing within a microcosm that in many respects is similar to the macrocosm. In other words, through our inner universe, we can connect to the outer universe, and through the divinities inside us, we cannot connect to the divinities of the universe. Indeed, this is the essential purpose of yoga and contemplative practices. Every aspect of the human body, down to the cellular level, represents Prakriti or the Field. Purusha, the Self, dwells in it as the support and illuminates the body. Hence, He is known as the illuminating Self (chaitanyatma). Their union in the microcosm of each jiva facilitates its life, birth, death, and rebirth until liberation is achieved. In the macrocosm, it results in the manifestation of Isvara, or the Cosmic Being, and His numerous manifestations. The whole creation, or the whole universe, is Isvara's cosmic body, illuminated by His radiance and filled with His presence. All the jivas and all the objective reality they experience internally and externally are also a part of His Cosmic Form only.

Isvara or Saguna Brahman is the first to manifest mysteriously from the equally mysterious Brahman, the Zero, just as the number one emerges from zero. Hence, in Sanskrit, zero (shunya) aptly describes the state of the unmanifested Brahman (asambhuta). It is the condition of Isvara, the One, before His existence or manifestation (sambhuta). Like zero, which is the starting point of all numbers, the unmanifested Brahman is the starting point of all existence. However, He does not participate in creation, nor is He the Creator. The creator is Isvara, the One. Just as numbers do not arise from zero but from number one only through additions, divisions, subtractions, and multiplications, the whole creation does not arise from Brahma, the zero, but from Isvara and His Shaktis. Just as number one is the creator of all numbers, digits, and integers, including fractions and negative numbers, Isvara is the creator of all diversity in existence. Just as number one exists in all other numbers, including fractions and negative numbers, Isvara, along with His Prakriti, remains hidden in every aspect of His creation. Furthermore, just as the value of any number increases significantly when you place one before it, you have a better chance of achieving peace, happiness, and liberation in your life by following Isvara, the One, putting Him before everything in your life, and worshipping Him with exclusive devotion (eka bhakti).

As a subjective reality, the number one also symbolizes Atman, the individual Self. Atman has the same attributes as Brahman. Just as Atman supports all jivas (living beings) from within, the number one supports all other numbers from within them. Like Atman, it is hidden in every other number. It is the essence of the eternal One. Hindu scholars are not unanimous about the relationship between Atman and Brahman. All agree that both share the same essence and bliss consciousness, but disagree when discussing their origin and relationship. According to monistic (Advaita) schools, Brahman and Atman are the same reality, and in the end, Atman becomes Brahman. The dualistic (Dvaita) schools believe that the two are distinct and that though they are the same, in essence, they never unite but remain distinct forever. According to them, an individual soul may achieve self-realization but would continue to exist eternally as a separate self.

Numerically, the number one may not have the range of zero in symbolizing Brahman, but it shares many of the latter's qualities. Like Saguna Brahman, who is the creator of all empirical reality, one is truly the creator of all other numbers. As the one Supreme Brahman becomes many in creation, one becomes many through addition and multiplication, and then resides within them. It is also different from zero because it has attributes, specific form, quantity, quality, specificity, and value. However, it is not eternal because, like Isvara or Saguna Brahman, it dissolves into zero or nothingness when subtracted from itself or when it comes into contact with zero during a multiplication.

One also symbolizes the state of nonduality, the oneness of existence that is hidden in all of creation beyond the veil of delusion and duality. The state of oneness is also the subjective state of both Brahman and Atman, in which all distinctions, divisions, duality, or separation between the known and the knower, the object and the subject, the self and the non-self, or the objective reality come to an end. It is the state in which one alone exists by oneself, illumined by the Self, immersed in the Self, permanent, unchanging, and unmoving. It is the state of "I am I am" in which "I," the objective self, disappears to become "I, " the subjective Self in the absolute state.

References

1. Westcott, W. W. (1911). *Numbers, their occult power and mystic virtues* (3rd ed.). Theosophical Publishing Society.

Two, Dvi

Unlike number one, whose base form (prātipadika) changes in singular, dual, or plural forms, the number two (Dvi) in Sanskrit is always used as a dual. It makes sense since number two refers to pairs and never more or less. However, its base form changes with grammatical genders (ling) and cases (vibhakti), as shown in the tables below.

Case	Masculine	Feminine	Neuter	Singular	Dual	Plural
Prathama	Dvau	Dvai	Dvai	—	Dvau	—
Dvitiya	Dvau	Dvai	Dvao	—	Dvau	—
Tritiya	Dvābhyām	Dvābhyām	Dvābhyām	—	Dvābhyām	—
Chaturtha	Dvābhyām	Dvābhyām	Dvābhyām	—	Dvābhyām	—
Panchami	Dvābhyām	Dvābhyām	Dvābhyām	—	Dvābhyām	—
Shashti	Dvayoh	Dvayoh	Dvayoh	—	Dvayoh	—
Saptami	Dvayoh	Dvayoh	Dvayoh	—	Dvayoh	—

In worldly life, two denotes company, friendship, relationship, equal parts, pairs, conflict, division, secondary, inferior, separation, and the replication of something. In some respects, two is more desirable than one, as in having twofold wealth, strength, or influence. In Nature, most things are found in pairs. For example, we have day and night, the earth and the sky, joy and sorrow, male and female, black and white, far and near, light and darkness, body and soul, good and evil, knowledge and ignorance, heat and cold, friendship and enmity, love and hate, and so on. The Hermetics identified this as the principle of polarity, according to which "everything is dual, everything has two poles, and everything has its pair of opposites." The postulated that the polarities are similar in nature but different in degree [1]. Hence, they believed that they could be reconciled and reduced to one, the state of nonduality. Everything comes in pairs, the twins of existence, born from the same reality, the Universal Mind, and joined at the hip. Chaldeans believed that the number two represents the sacred sanctuary, space, or silence, the first number, to separate from the Divine. Greek philosophers thought that it symbolized the "fountain of symphony and harmony," the interval between God and His creation, and between the unity and the diversity that manifests in the world as the multitude. The Egyptians depicted it as two serpents in a tight embrace producing an egg, the world [2]. In Christianity, the number two represents Adam and Eve, the New Testament, the two tables of the Law, the two witnesses of Resurrection, and more.

In nature, the number two represents balance and symmetry. For example, we have two eyes, two ears, two lips, two lungs, two kidneys, two hands, and two feet. We have two sides to our bodies and two hemispheres in our brains. They make the human body complete and perfect. Many plant seeds are divided into two halves. Everything has two sides, back and front, or the visible side and the hidden side. Thus, the number two complements and makes things full. Numerically, two is greater than one, but in life, it is often the opposite. Who wants to be a number two in a competition? Number one is the winning position or the mark of a champion. In those situations, number two means the second best, the runner-up, or not up to the mark. In some situations, having two is better than having one. The number two also represents the doubling of some quality, trait, or quantity. A person can be doubly evil, cruel, or hostile (dvisatah). The Bhagavadgita calls them cruel haters and the lowest of humans.

Someone said that no one remembers the number twos or threes, and it requires a lot of effort to be number one. Being number two in life is a challenge, and no one likes to remain a number two forever. Someone also said that it requires a lot of courage, grit, heart, and strength to remain number two for a long time and endure all the frustration and disappointment that comes with it. In marital relationships, historically, women have remained number twos for a long time before they decided to change the equation. However, in a chain of command, number twos command respect. For instance, in temples, you must approach the number twos (the priests) to make offerings and reach the number one (God). Although it is not a cherished goal or a desirable option sometimes, we have to go through the number three or two positions to reach the number one position. Nevertheless, we must be glad that life always gives us second chances. Life is better when we are not alone for a long time, when we have another person to speak to or share our happy moments, or when we have more than one option to make decisions or exercise our freedom. Life is also better when you have two streams of income, twofold wealth, or twofold success. However, no one likes a two-faced person or double-speak. Two can be a problem when people with opposite temperaments meet, marry, work together, or are forced to spend time together. It is said that sometimes life brings them together to teach each of them important lessons in tolerance, patience, and endurance.

Number two also has great mystic or spiritual significance in Hinduism. It represents Prakriti, Shakti, the body, duality, ego, Death, the ancestral heaven, the mid-region, creation, the householder phase, the pursuit of wealth, Samaveda, and many other things because of their origin or status in the order of creation. The Supreme Being, Isvara, who manifests from Brahman and goes by different names, is not just the first to manifest in creation; He is also without a second (advitiya) and without duality (advandva). If number one represents Him, number two represents Prakriti and Her creation or manifestation. Prakriti is His second half, his dynamic energy principle, which is chiefly responsible for all the manifestations. By meditating on the First and establishing oneself in it, one attains liberation, but by becoming involved with the second, one remains stuck in samsara.

Symbolically and philosophically, number two represents the state of duality, which we experience objectively through our minds and the senses. It also symbolizes the duality of Purusha and Prakriti (the creator God and Nature), Brahman and Atman as two distinct entities, the knower and the known, the subject and the object, the doer and the deed, the self and the not-self, the bhutatman (ego or physical self) and the antaratman (inner Self), Siva and Shakti, Vishnu and Lakshmi, Brahma and Saraswathi, the earth and the sky, cause and effect, the day and the night, the heaven and the hell, the good and evil, the right and wrong, knowledge and ignorance, higher knowledge and lower knowledge, life and death, illusion and illumination and mortality and immortality. In the Bhagavadgita, Lord Krishna says he declared two types of disciplines (dvividha nishta) in the past: Jnana yoga for the seekers of knowledge (Samkhyas) and Karma yoga for those who are bound by their obligatory duties (karma yogis). The Upanishads declare two types of knowledge: higher knowledge (vidya) and lower knowledge (avidya). The Isa Upanishad declares that both are necessary to attain liberation. Two is the first to manifest from one in creation. Without two, further diversity is not possible. Without the other (the male or the female), life itself is not possible.

The positive and negative aspects of life always balance each other. Creation itself arises from their union. Everything in creation has at least two sides, male and female, the right and left, up and down, inside and outside. The mind and senses have two modes: an outward and an inward mode. Without these modes, the mind cannot attain stability or balance. When the mind and senses are outgoing, we experience life and its modifications and disturbances. When they are withdrawn, we experience peace and equanimity. Brahman Himself understood the need for a second entity, an opposite, or a mirror-self of Himself during creation. The Upanishads state that when the Creator woke from a long sleep and opened His eyes, He was not happy being alone. Therefore, He created a second of everything: a wife for the husband, a female for the male, a body for the soul, heaven for earth, bondage for free souls, liberation for bound souls, knowledge for the ignorant, consciousness for unconscious matter, an object for the subject, and so on. From that single seed of thought ensued all creation, as reflections in the Field of Prakriti. The emergence of two from one is the starting point of our existence, and also the starting point of our problems of mortality and suffering. How to resolve the two into one and the one into zero is a puzzle or paradox we must address by finding our source, either by attaining the one (the Self or self-realization) within ourselves and dissolving the dualities and objectivity in Brahman, the Zero (Nirvana).

In worldly life, we are drawn to pairs of opposites due to attraction and aversion. Desires and attachments arising from them subject us to ignorance and delusion and keep us bound to samsara. Our suffering and bondage to ignorance and mortality are symbolically represented in the predicament of Adam and Eve after they are cast away from heaven in the Biblical story of Genesis. In Vedanta, it is philosophically explained as bondage to ignorance and earthly life due to desires and attachments. In both situations, the result is suffering and our continued existence in the world of Death. Karma is the poison that enters our lives when we fall under the spell of desires and attachments and engage in desire-ridden actions to fulfill them. We are always caught in the dance of the two opposites: Dharma and Adharma, karma and akarma, attraction and aversion, good and evil, bondage and liberation, happiness and sorrow, and the Self and the not-self.

Two can also be a source of confusion, conflict, and ambiguity, especially when we cannot decide between them or know which is better for us. Hence, our scriptures suggest that we must practice detachment and renunciation of desires to purify our intelligence and cultivate discernment. The Bhagavadgita recommends that one should cultivate skillfulness in yoga with a resolute mind (vyavasayātmika buddhi) and one-pointed intelligence to think with discernment, make right decisions, and avoid falling into delusion and self-destruction through desire-ridden actions. In the second chapter (2.46), Lord Krishna says, *"When your intelligence, which is troubled by the conflicting statements of the Vedas, becomes stable and firm in self-absorption, then you will attain yoga."*

Hinduism believes in the concept of the twice-born (dvija), which means human beings must undergo two births in their lives to qualify for spiritual practice and attain liberation. The first is a natural birth, and the second is a spiritual birth. In their first birth, human beings open their eyes and become aware of the world around them, their minds and bodies, and their worldly existence. At this stage, their existence is comparable to that of an animal (pasu), as they are primarily driven by their animal or lower nature, desires, attachments, instincts, impulses, passions, emotions, egoism, and delusion. By pursuing worldly desires and aims (Dharma, Artha, and Kama), they become bound to samsara, the cycle of births and deaths. In the second birth, which may happen due to initiation by a spiritual teacher, they open their eyes to their essential nature or higher nature, and become aware of their true identity as a Pure Self and their true or ultimate purpose, which is liberation (Moksha). By overcoming desires and attachments and renouncing worldly life, they engage in spiritual practice and attain immortality or the state of Brahman. Those who are born twice are thus known as Dvija, the twice-born. However, the Aitareya Upanishad describes three births during a soul's transmigration. The first birth is when a departed soul returns from the ancestral world through rainwater and enters his father's body through food. The second birth is when he enters his mother's womb through his father's body. The third birth is when he is born from the womb. The Vedas have a different take on this. They consider the people who are born in the higher castes to be twice-born. However, the law books warn that if they do not live righteously, performing their obligatory duties as ordained by the texts, they will not be considered twice-born.

Number two is also used both literally and symbolically in the following instances.

- The concept of dvandva refers to any pair of opposite sexes, conditions, qualities, natures, dualities, or the double of anything. It also refers to strife, quarrel, rivalry, or dispute between two persons or groups. In Sanskrit grammar, dvandva samasa means any coordinate compound word in which both the words are equally important and necessary, as in Ramakrishna, sukhadukha, etc. A duel or fight between two opponents having different aims or goals is called dvandva yuddham. Having conflicting attitudes toward a person or thing is often expressed as dvandva bhava. Dvandva Niti refers to the policy of using dual strategies to resolve problems, conflicts, or disputes.
- The number two symbolizes the sun and the moon, the two celestial bodies visible to the naked eye. The eyes of gods such as Vishnu, Shiva, or Kartikeya are often compared to them
- Number two also represents associated pairs such as the physical and spiritual realms, and dual qualities that go together, such as love and compassion, beauty and grace, knowledge and wisdom, and so on.

- Number two has greater value than one, but in real life, sometimes it carries things of lesser importance. Number one is unique (advitiya), but number two is secondary (dvitiya). Anything that is of lesser importance in status, value, succession, or position is secondary or a second. For example, number one is associated with a winner and number two with a runner, the person who also ran (and lost).
- In Hinduism, a woman or a wife is historically considered inferior to men. The tradition ordains obligatory duties primarily for men and recognizes them as the hosts (yajamana) of the Vedic sacrifice, while women play a secondary role as co-hosts. Hence, in marriage relationships, a woman is designated as the second (dvitiya). However, in today's world, women's position and roles are changing, and women are taking lead roles in many matters.
- One represents unity, two denotes division. It is the starting point of all categories, classes, and divisions. The Vedas are divided into two sections: Karmakanda (the ritual portion containing the knowledge of sacrifices) and Jnanakanda (the spiritual part containing the knowledge of the Self). Both are necessary for the householders to pursue the four aims of human life and fulfill their obligatory duties.
- Hindu texts such as the Bhagavadgita and the Upanishads identify two paths (dvipatha) by which embodied souls depart from here after death. One leads to the ancestral world, and the other to the immortal world. The former results in rebirth and the latter in immortality. They are also known as the inferior and the superior paths.
- Two is associated with any bidirectional movement, such as progression and regression, evolution and involution, upward and downward movements, etc. The mind and senses are subject to this polarity. They have outward (pravritti) and inward (nivrtti) modes. The former results in restlessness, modifications of the mind, and instability. The latter, when practiced with self-control and detachment, results in mental stability, peace, and equanimity.

- Before the current number system was devised, the alphasyllabic symbol for two used to be 'Kha,' the second letter in the Ka group (varga) of the Sanskrit alphabet. In Vedic numerology, the symbol may still be in use for calculations. The letter also represents the sun and sky.
- In Hindu philosophy, two represents the Dvaita doctrine of Vedanta, according to which a fundamental and eternal duality exists between God and His creation, between God and jivas, between Atman (individual Self) and Brahman (the Supreme Self). The duality persists even after the jivas attain liberation. In contrast, Advaita, the school of nondualism, holds that the absolute, supreme reality of Brahman alone is real, and the duality arising from His creation is a temporary illusion or projection. The illusion leads to the mistaken notion that the physical self is the real self or that the apparent world is real and everlasting.
- The number two symbolizes the second chapter of the Bhagavadgita, known as Samkhya Yoga, meaning the Yoga of Self-Knowledge. Some regard it as a summary of the entire scripture.
- Number two is also associated with Ganesha. He said to possess two faces or forms: a primeval form and a manifested form, with which he can see inwardly and outwardly. Hence, he has the epithet of Dvimukhayana, the Lord with two faces. He also has two mothers: Parvathi and Jahnavi. Hence, he is called Dvaimatura, the Lord with two mothers. Jarasandha of the Mahabharata is also known as Dvaimatura because he was born in two halves from the wombs of two mothers. Both halves were joined magically into a complete body by a demoness named Jara. Hence, he became known as Jarasandha.
- In some instances, two denotes privacy or exclusivity. For example, dvandvalapa in Sanskrit refers to a private or exclusive conversation between two persons.
- Two often represents deception, falsehood, duplicity, inconsistency, etc. For example, double-face (dvimukha), double-

tongue (dvijihva), and double meaning (dvandvabhava) are a few popular words in usage.
- Two is sometimes used to denote anything in excess of or double the quality or intensity, as in the case of double happiness, double profit, double strength, etc. It is also often used to denote "either or" situations. For example, dvandva dukkha refers to pain arising from dualities or opposites, such as heat and cold or friendship and enmity.
- Two also denotes a strong bond, relationship, or association. Some Hindu gods and goddesses are often paired because of their identical nature, affinity, or historical connection. The two Asvins are always invoked together. Other popular pairs mentioned in the Puranas and Epics are Hari-Hara, Shiva-Shakti, Nara-Narayana, Krishna-Arjuna, Yama-Yami, Rama-Lakshmana, Rahu-Ketu, etc.
- In some instances, two represents a limit, boundary, or threshold. Dvandatitha refers to a condition or a yogi who transcends the dualities and remains established in equanimity and sameness.

Reference

1. Three Initiates. 1908. The Kybalion: A Study of the Hermetic Philosophy of Ancient Egypt and Greece. Chicago: The Yogi Publication Society.
2. Westcott, W. Wynn. 1911. Numbers: Their Occult Power and Mystic Virtues. London: Theosophical Publishing Society.

Three, Triah

Unlike the numbers one and two, the number three in Sanskrit is always used in a plural sense. However, like the others, its form may vary according to each case (vibhakti) and gender (ling), as shown below.

Vibhakti (Case)	Masculine (Pullingam)	Feminine (Streelingam)	Neuter (Napunsaklingam)
Prathama	Trayaha	Tisrah	Trini
Dvitiya	Treen	Tisrah	Trini
Tritiya	Tribhih	Tisrbhih	Tribhih
Chaturthi	Tribhyah	Tisrbhyah	Tribhyah
Panchami	Tribhyah	Tisrbhyah	Tribhyah
Shasthi	Trayanaam	Tisrnaam	Trayanaam
Saptami	Trishu	Tisrsu	Trishu

Among the digits (numbers 1 to 9), three is the second odd number after one. In life, it represents the Triad: the threefold nature, aspect, action, mode, quality, or state of anything, and symbolizes balance, harmony, symmetry, and the progression of the things found in Nature. Although zero and the circle are commonly known to symbolize cyclical movements or processes, the triangle, formed by the geometric unity of three lines connected at each end, also represents cyclical or sequential movements. Three is the first prime number that forms a geometric shape, the triangle. Pythagoras, who believed that the principles that govern numbers also determine the realities, principles, or truths of the empirical world, conceived number one as a Monad, number two as a Dyad, and number three as a Triad. According to his teachings, the Monad, represented by a dot, symbolizes God, the Supreme Being, and the ultimate unity of all existences; the Dyad, represented by a line, symbolizes twoness, otherness, duality, materiality, and pairs of opposites, with the base-line serving as the connecting link between those opposites, while the Triad, represented by a triangle, symbolizes the relationship between three equal or unequal points, aspects, or entities. In other words, the number three serves as the connecting or balancing link between the dualities or opposites of our empirical existence. It also represents neutrality, the middle ground, for example, the state which is neither hot nor cold, neither happiness nor sorrowfulness, neither rich nor poor, neither far nor near, and so on.

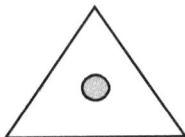

Number three is unique because it is the first odd number among the digits (numbers 1 to 9) that can be divided into three equal parts by one and two unequal parts by two. Geometrically, it represents a triangle with two equal parts and one unequal part. Symbolically, it denotes balance, stability, and symmetry. The Pythagorean triad symbolizes a triangle with two shorter sides and one longer side. In mathematical terms, they represent a set of three positive integers (a, b, c) that satisfy the equation: $a^2 + b^2 = c^2$. One of the numbers is always even, while the other two are odd. This means that the sum of the squares of the shorter sides of a right-angled triangle is always equal to the square of the hypotenuse.

Triangles play an important role in architectural designs and engineering. They symbolize the harmony and perfection found in creation. In worldly life, triangles can be troublesome, especially in personal and romantic relationships, if three people compete for equal attention. You may have heard of the tension and complications that such relationships can create. There is a saying that two is company and three is a crowd. The number three also symbolizes anything that has a beginning, a middle, and an end. By this analogy, it represents life itself since it has a beginning, a middle, and an end. Similarly, three also symbolizes these triads: creation, preservation, and destruction, birth, existence, and death, sunrise, midday, and evening, the earth, the mid-region, and heaven, and any creative process that begins with planning or conception continues during its execution and ends with its completion.

In Hindu philosophy, the number three symbolizes the material manifestation (the worlds and beings) that arises from Isvara at the beginning of creation. Zero represents the enigma and completeness of Brahman. The number one corresponds to the singularity and supremacy of Isvara, the Lord of the Universe, who is the first and foremost to arise from Brahman. The number two symbolizes Prakriti or Nature, an essential aspect of Isvara that sets in motion the whole creation. Prakriti is also responsible for the universal twos or the pairs of opposites, such as heat and cold, happiness and sorrow, day and night, and so on. The whole manifestation (Viraj), consisting of all the worlds and beings, is the third reality to manifest. It is illuminated by Isvara, since it lacks illumination of its own. It is the sum of the triple aspects of existence: the Supreme Self, the embodied Selves (jivatmas), and Prakriti, who represents all the materiality and objectivity they experience. In the jivas, the triangularity is well represented by the physical self (the gross body), the mental self (subtle body), and the spiritual Self. In the triangle of a jiva's existence, the Self serves as the baseline, the gross and subtle bodies represent the two sides, while Prakriti and Isvara serve as the dot (bindu) and space, respectively, uniting and supporting it. Alternatively, we may also say that in the microcosm of each jiva, one represents the Knower of the Field, two represents the Field of Prakriti, and three represents the ignorant and bound jiva who experiences the illusion of the duality of subject and object and separation, which leads to egoism, desires, attachments, delusion and bondage.

Thus, creation (the Triad) manifests from the union of Purusha (Monad) and Prakriti (Dyad). One of the things that they manifest together is Rta or Rtam, which is the name given in the Vedas to the universal rhythm or order and regularity that is hidden in creation. It is the underlying rhythm or pulse of the universe that operates in the same manner as the rhythms in musical meters. It manifests itself in many ways as the orderly progression of time and events. In the human body, Rta is responsible for the biological cycle, the progression of life from birth to death, the aging process that is tied to age and other factors, and the sounds that arise from speech or singing. In the macrocosm, one can discern its working in the recurring patterns of days and nights, months and years, the movements of planets, constellations, the sun and moon, the movement of seasons, among others. The number three also symbolizes this Rta, since it is an essential aspect of creation.

Creation cannot be chaotic or disorderly. It is a projection of God, who is a perfect Being, complete in all respects. It cannot be imperfect because imperfection cannot arise from perfection. Any imperfection or failure we may discern in creation is God's willful concealment of perfection for a reason, part of a grand design to ensure the universal Rta or order of things, which we may not understand because of our limited faculties. However, we can see this regularity and orderliness (Rta) in every aspect of creation, from atoms to the galaxies, from genes, chromosomes, and DNA molecules to ecosystems, from the heavens to the earth, and within our minds and bodies, manifesting itself as an orderly progression of time and events, an arrangement of things and energies and as beauty, symmetry, regularity, and harmony. It is the dance of Siva in his cosmic grandeur. Despite the seemingly chaotic process of creation and manifestation of the universe, we can discern in it an orderly progression of events, a certain rhythm, and the predictability of the movement and constitution of objects and beings. It points to the likelihood that mathematical principles and algorithms are hidden in every aspect of God's creation because He personifies order, regularity, beauty, perfection, symmetry, and harmony.

Amidst the chaos unleashed by the primal force, what is the first orderly process that manifests in creation and lays the foundation for its Rta or rhythm? It is the universal order, the triangular process that heralds the beginning, the middle, and the end of all life forms and inanimate objects. They happen recurringly and repetitively as life goes on and as beings are caught in the dualities and the impermanence of their mortal existence. These three phases of creation, the trident of Nature's inviolable force, happen in the mortal world ruled by Death due to her triple functions: Creation, Preservation, and Destruction. They set in motion a number of other processes, again, each with a beginning, a middle, and an end, and each serving as a cause or an effect or both. They are personified in the Hindu pantheon as the Trinity of gods: Brahma, Vishnu, and Shiva. Brahma is the creator, Vishnu is the preserver, and Siva is the destroyer. They themselves personify the working of Rta and act as its highest and ultimate upholders, enforcers, and guardians, ensuring that creation progresses as designed and willed without major disruptions.

Thus, the cosmic triangle of creation is personified by the three deities (trideva), Vishnu serving as the baseline and the other two as the sidelines, with Isvara as the dot (bindu) in the middle and Brahman as the space in between, serving as their source and support. Working together in perfect harmony as the forces of Rta, they ensure the balance, order, stability, and continuity of the whole creation for the duration of each cycle. Although devotees worship them as distinct deities, each with specific names and forms, they are connected internally with each other through Brahman (Purusha, Prakriti), and represent the hidden triangle that pervades and encompasses the whole creation. Each of them has one aspect of Purusha (number one), one aspect of Shakti (number two), and one aspect of their own nature (number three), connected to each through the pure consciousness of Brahman, the dot. Their essential nature, the third aspect, is related to their functions, duties, individual qualities, and attributes, which determine their role, significance, and place (Rta) in the universal order of creation. However, in their highest, purest, and absolute aspects, they represent Brahman (both manifested and unmanifested) and act independently as Isvara in their respective spheres, performing the triple functions of creation, preservation, and destruction. In other words, the Trinity of gods is different but not different, distinct but not distinct, distinct like the lines in the triangle, but connected internally and working in harmony. Therefore, when we speak about them, it is difficult to know whether we speak about them specifically or about Brahman or Isvara, whom they represent in their ultimate essence.

Brahma is the creator god. He is Prajapati, the lord of beings, who creates beautiful forms through his divine mind. In him, divine will and energy work in perfect harmony to manifest his divine intention instantaneously. Vishnu is the preserver. He upholds and preserves the Rta (order, harmony, rhythm, and regularity) of the universe by nourishing it and protecting it from the disruptors, the evil Asuras. He also ensures that the worlds, grahas (planets), and other celestial objects remain in their respective spheres or houses and move as ordained according to His divine will. Shiva is the destroyer. He ensures the Rta of the universe by cleaning, purifying, destroying, and transforming beings and objects as Time (Kala) or Death according to their nature and destinies. He destroys or removes whatever can potentially disturb the universal Rta by consuming it as His food and thereby facilitates the renewal and regeneration of the worlds and their beings. He also helps them in their spiritual transformation and evolution through their transmigration so that at some point in time, they will return to their original and essential nature and escape from samsara. In the end, He dissolves or withdraws everything into Himself, into the vast unknown (the zero), and remains in that state until the next cycle of creation.

Number three aptly symbolizes Lord Shiva. He is not only the third in the Trinity of gods but also personifies the three in many other ways. For example, he is known as the deity with three eyes (Trinetra). With his third eye, which adorns the center of his forehead like a shining jewel, he imparts the knowledge of the Self and liberation to his worshippers and destroys their ignorance and delusion. He carries a trident called Trishul or triayudha (trident), which is a transformative and destructive weapon. With it, he protects the pious and the pure and destroys the evil ones. He is the lord of the three modes (Trigunadhipati): sattva, rajas, and tamas, with which he deludes beings and subjects them to animal nature, imparting to them the triple impurities of egoism, desires, and delusion. He is the lord with three braids (Trijatadhari), which symbolize his three Shaktis (creative, supportive, and destructive forces or energies) that assist Him in his duties. He is also extolled as the lord of the three worlds (Trilokeswara): the earth, heaven, and the underworld, or the earth, the mid-region, and heaven, the knower of the three worlds (Trilokajnani), and the knower of three divisions of time (Trikalajnani): the past, present, and future.

Number three also symbolically represents the sacred syllable AUM in its vocative and diagrammatic aspects. In the images, AUM is depicted as having three curves representing the three states of consciousness (wakeful, dream, and deep sleep states). The dot at the top represents Brahman, the transcendental Shiva consciousness, the zero. When uttered loudly, it produces three sounds, A, U, and M, followed by silence. Individually, they symbolize the triple worlds, and collectively they represent space (akasa) in which they are located and through which our speech (sounds) travels to Brahman, who represents the silence beyond them. The Mandukya Upanishad explains the symbolism of AUM in great detail. It states that the lower curve in the diagrammatic representation of AUM signifies the outgoing wakeful consciousness (prvritti); the middle part represents the incoming dream consciousness; the upper curve represents the static consciousness of the deep sleep state, which is an indeterminate state filled with stupor or unconsciousness induced by tamas; while the dot or the diamond above the upper curve represents the turya or the pure consciousness of Atman itself. Like a dot, it is unlimited and indeterminate, and like a diamond, it is strong, stable, and indestructible. This fourth state of consciousness, symbolized by the zero or the dot, is neither inner nor outer and neither consciousness nor unconsciousness. It is self-luminous, illuminates everything within its reach, and exists here and beyond, alone and without any agencies and dependencies. The three states of consciousness are also represented by the three sounds A, U, and M, whereas the silence that follows them represents turya, the fourth state. When we utter the syllable AUM repetitively, focusing on the silence that follows, it will gradually awaken us into the fourth state of pure, transcendental consciousness.

The Sanskrit word for the number three is Tri (thri). This alone proves that several Indian numerals have been adapted into other languages outside India with modifications. The Vedas were originally three. Therefore, they were called the threefold knowledge (triaividya). Lord Shiva is known as Trayambaka, meaning the god with three eyes, and Parvati as Trayambika, the goddess with three eyes. The sacred goddess Ganga is known as Trimargana since she flows through three worlds.

As we have discussed before, the number three symbolizes many things in Hinduism. Most popularly, it is used to denote, describe, or symbolize three of something: ways, means, types, qualities, parts, objects, manifestations, forms, methods, actions, attributes, achievements, philosophical concepts, ritual actions, realities, deities, and more. They convey strength, unity, diversity, importance, options, power, association, hidden connections, relationship, etc. The following are a few important examples found in Hindu scriptures.

- Trividya: Three types of knowledge or knowledge of the triple Vedas, namely Rigveda, Yajurveda, and Samaveda. The Brahmana who knows them is called Trivedi.
- Trividhi: Three ways of being or doing something. The word is used in different contexts. Trividhi karma refers to three types of karma: Sanchita (accumulated), Prarabdha (karma currently fructifying), and Kriyamana (ongoing and shaping the future). Trividhi bhakti means three types of devotion induced by the triple modes of Sattva, Rajas, and Tamas, respectively. Trividhi vidya refers to three types of knowledge: worldly (apara), spiritual (para), and transcendental (parapara). Trividha has a similar meaning and is used in some contexts.
- Tretayuga: The third epoch (yuga) in the current great epoch (mahayuga), which witnessed the Mahabharata war and ended with the conclusion of the incarnation of Lord Krishna. It was followed by Kaliyuga, the current and final epoch, at the end of which there will be a reset and another great epoch will begin.
- Trishul: The trident of Lord Shiva. It symbolizes many things: the triple forms of Shakti, the triple modes of Nature, the triple functions of God, the remover of the triple impurities, the triple Nadis, etc.
- Trishakti: The three powers of Shakti, namely Iccha (will or intention), Jnana (knowledge), and Kriya (action). They are the three fundamental manifestations of Prakriti or Shakti described in many texts of Hinduism, especially Shaivism and Tantra. Iccha Shakti represents divine will or intention. Jnana Shakti represents the power of knowing, cognition, awareness, insight, and intuition. Kriya Shakti represents the power of action, movement, and transformation that translates the divine will into reality. The first one is the spark of desire. The second one is the knowledge or wisdom that shapes it into a specific form or outcome. The third one transforms it into reality. Together, they complete the cycle of creation.
- The three entities of creation: In Shaivism, Pati, Pasa, Pasu represent the foundational aspects of creation, representing the relationship between God, the embodied souls, and the forces

that define their relationship and bind the souls to samsara. Pati is Shiva, the Lord of all existence. Pasu is the deluded jiva, embodied soul, caught in samsara. Pasas are the desires and attachments that bind the jivas and keep them deluded and bound to the cycle of births and deaths.

- The triple means of knowing: The Vedanta philosophy recognizes Sravanam, Mananam, and Nidhidhyasanam as the triple means of knowing, learning, and self-realization. Sravanam means hearing or listening to the sacred teachings. Mananam means remembering, recollecting, or contemplating what has been learned or heard. Nidhidhyasana means becoming absorbed in that thought process, until a yogi experiences that knowledge directly without the intervention of the mind or its agents.

- The three aspects of the Goddess: In Shaivism and Tantra, Para, Parapara, and Apara, are the triple forms or aspects of Shakti. In creation, they represent Shakti's triple states: transcendental, subtle, and gross. In the jivas, they represent her three potencies, realities, and types of awareness: the knower, the means of knowing, and the known.

- The three potencies of Shakti: Anuttara Shakti, the power of awareness; Ananda Shakti, the power of bliss; and Iccha Shakti, the power of will, represent the three forms of Shakti hidden in the consciousness of each jiva. They facilitate the progression of jivas from ignorance and delusion to knowledge, bliss, liberation, and the power to manifest divine will.

- Trimārga: The three main spiritual paths of liberation. In Hinduism, jnana, karma, and sannyasa yogas represent the triple paths of liberation that lead beings toward oneness with the Supreme Self. Karma yoga involves the performance of obligatory duties in devotion to God and His creation. Jnana yoga involves studying the scriptures and acquiring knowledge to realize one's divine nature and abide by it. Sannyasa yoga involves the renunciation of worldly desires and attachments, cultivation of detachment and indifference, performing actions as a sacrifice, and remaining absorbed in contemplation until duality and delusion are overcome.

- Trikarma: Three types of karma or obligatory duty. Hindu law books prescribe sacrifice, study, and charity as the three fundamental duties of a devout Brahmana who follows the Grihastashrama Dharma as a householder. They lead to knowledge, purification, and enlightenment.
- Triguna: The triple modes of Nature. In Hindu philosophy, Sattva, Rajas, and Tamas represent the triple modes by which Nature induces desires and attachments of various kinds and manifests diverse natures, behaviors, and attitudes. Under their influence, jivas engage in desire-ridden actions and remain bound to samsara. God is considered the Lord of the gunas (trigunadhipati). Those who pursue liberation must transcend the gunas to cultivate sameness and freedom from karma.
- Trichit: Three layers of fuel arrangement or sacrificial altars mentioned in the Satapatha Brahmana and Katyayana Srauta Sutra in connection with Vedic sacrifices. Each layer in a sacrificial altar symbolizes a particular aspect of existence, world, or sphere. According to some interpretations, they represent the three layers of Hindu temple architecture or the three divisions of time, past, present, and future. They also refer to the three layers or aspects of Nature: light, fire, and darkness representing the triple aspects of creation and consciousness, often symbolized as the Trinity (Vishnu, Brahma, and Shiva), the triple layers of consciousness (waking, dream, and deep sleep), the triple modes purity, passion, and ignorance or inertia (Sattva, Rajas, and Tamas), and so on.
- Tristali: Three sacred places of great significance, namely Kashi, Prayag, and Gaya. Each of them has a long history and spiritual importance. Kashi, the oldest living city in the world, is a gateway to liberation. Prayag is the site of Triveni Sangam, where three rivers (Ganga, Yamuna, and Saraswati) meet, and where the most sacred Hindu festival, Kumbh Mela, is celebrated once every 12 years. Gaya is associated with ancestral rites for the return, rebirth, or liberation of departed souls.
- Tridandam: In some Hindu traditions, especially Shaivism and Vaishnavism, renunciants carry a sacred staff consisting of

three staves known as tridanda. Those who carry them are known as tridandins. The three staves represent the threefold reality (pati, pasu, pasa, or God, Nature, and jiva), the triple modes, and the threefold control (the mind, body, and actions or speech).
- The three states of a being: In Hinduism, creation manifests at three levels: gross, subtle, and transcendental. They also manifest in each jiva. The gross and subtle aspects belong to the domain of Prakriti and are subject to modifications. The transcendental aspect belongs to Purusha, the Self or Brahman. It is not subject to modifications, but the doorway to liberation and immortality.
- Trikaya: In Mahayana Buddhism, the Trikaya doctrine describes the three bodies of the Buddha: the Dharma body (Dharmakaya), the Bliss body (Sambhogakaya), and the Manifested body (Nirmanakaya). They represent the physical and the transcendental aspects of the Buddha and point to his existence in both states simultaneously.
- Trikala: In Hinduism, Time is an aspect or manifestation of God. It is also known as Death. The three divisions of Time, past, present, and future, known as Trikala, exist only in creation but not in the absolute state of Brahman. These divisions arise due to Maya and the memorial mind.
- Triganah: In the Vedic tradition, a householder has the obligatory duty of pursuing four chief aims known as the Purusharthas, namely Dharma, Artha, Kama, and Moksha. Of them, the first three aims are known as the trivarga.
- Trisandhya: This refers to the popular practice of offering three daily prayers to the sun or other gods at dawn, noon, and dusk in Hinduism, with its origins in the Vedas and the Vedic tradition. Devotees offer prayers from the Vedas, uttering important mantras such as the Gayatri, the Narayana or Shiva Mantras, and purification mantras. The morning prayers typically include offerings of water if worshippers take a public bath in a river or pond.
- Triloka: The Vedas describe a cosmology consisting of three worlds, Bhur, Bhuva, and Swaha, representing the upper,

middle, and lower worlds of God's creation and collectively referred to as Triloka or triple worlds. They are also known as Tribhuvana and Trijagati. Isvara is also known as the lord of the three worlds (Trilokeswara or Trilokadhipati).

- Tridhosha: According to Ayurveda, the human body is subject to three types of physical and mental disorders associated with the three fundamental energies of the body, vata (air or ether), pitta (fire and water), and kapha (earth and water). Ayurveda aims to balance these doshas through various treatments.
- Tripatham: Hinduism believes that three paths are designated for the embodied souls after they depart from this world according to their karma: The upward path that leads to the immortal heaven, the middle path that leads to a temporary stay in the ancestral heaven before returning to the world for rebirth, and the downward path that leads to hell or the underworld of Yama for punishment and expiation. It also means a place where three roads meet. Tripathagā is one of the epithets of Ganga.
- Tripada: Meaning "triple words, states, parts, or sections," Tripada has multiple references in Hinduism. It refers to one of the seven major Vedic meters, consisting of three octosyllabic sections in Sanskrit. The famous Gayatri mantra from the Rigveda (3.62.10) is composed in this meter. In Sanskrit grammar, a sentence structure made up of three words (padas) is also known by the same name. In Ayurveda, this term refers to a plant known for its healing properties. In Hindu spirituality, it denotes the triple functions of God: creation, preservation, and destruction, and the triple states of a jiva: the body, the mind, and the soul.
- Tripāda: According to the Bhagavata and Vishnu Puranas, Lord Vishnu incarnated as Vamana, at the request of the gods, and covered all of existence in three strides. With that, he left no option for Bali, a demon king, other than offering his head as a place for his foot, with which he pushed Bali down into the underworld. Thus, he is known as Tripāda, the Lord of the three strides.

- Tripundram: Lord Shiva's devotees customarily wear the mark of three horizontal lines on their foreheads to distinguish themselves and declare their devotion and allegiance. It is believed to protect them from the negative influences of the triple gunas and from the triple impurities of egoism, desires, and delusion, to which the jivas are subject and which are chiefly responsible for their bondage and suffering.
- Triputa: Meaning the triangle. This is an epithet of Durga, who, as Prakriti, personifies the whole manifested creation.
- Tripura: A collection of three cities of gold, silver, and iron built in the sky, air, and earth for demons by Maya that Lord Shiva ultimately burned down at the request of the gods.
- The three phases of life: Human life is divided into three phases: childhood, adulthood, and old age.
- The three types of breath: Usually, Hindu texts describe the Prana of five kinds. However, in some instances, only three are mentioned: the incoming breath (prana), the outgoing breath (udana), and the equalizing breath (samana).
- Triakshara: The mystic syllable Aum, represented by the three letters and three sounds, A, U, M.
- Trivarga: The three upper Varnas or classes (vargas) of humans. The Vedic society was originally divided into three vargas: Brahmana, Kshatriya, and Vaisya. The fourth class, Shudra, was added subsequently.
- Triveni Sangam: The confluence at Prayag, where the three sacred rivers, Ganga, Yamuna, and Saraswati, meet. It is also an important pilgrimage center and the place where the Maha Kumbh is celebrated.
- Trilinga: The three genders. Unlike English, Sanskrit has three grammatical genders (lingas), masculine, feminine, and neuter.
- Trika Shaivism: Also known as Kashmiri Shaivism, Trika aims to liberate humans through the intervention of the triple or the threefold Shaktis, Para, Parapara, and Apara. Trika refers to the three fundamental realities of existence: Shiva, Shakti, and Jiva. It has three core concepts: Pratyabhijna (awareness of one's Shiva nature), Spanda (the energy pulsating through the

universe and at the heart of all things and movements), and Krama, the sequential path to liberation.
- Epithets signifying three: Many epithets of prominent Hindu gods, such as Vishnu, Indra, and Shiva (the Trinity), are associated with the number three, such as Trinetra, Trilokeswara, Trigunadhipati, Trijata, Triadhipa, Tripati, Trivikrama, etc. The goddesses associated with them also often carry similar names, such as Tripureswari and Tripura Sundari.

Four, Chatur

Symbolically, the number four represents stability, symmetry, support, completeness, space, enclosure, ground, etc. Geometrically, it represents a square, or rectangle, or any form or shape in which four lines meet or cross each other. Four is an even number that can be divided into two or four equal parts and several unequal parts. It represents many aspects of everyday reality. In mathematics, addition (+), subtraction (−), multiplication (×), and division (÷) constitute the four elementary arithmetic operations. Four is a universal measure of time and space. Each day and year is divided into four parts. Minutes and hours are also measured in four quarters (chaturdamsha). The leap year comes once in four years. Each month has four weeks. Human life is divided into four parts (chaturavasta) in almost all cultures across the world: childhood (balyam), adolescence (kaumaram), adulthood (yauvanam), and old age (vrddhapyam). Each time cycle in Hinduism is divided into four great epochs (yugas): Satyayuga, Tretayuga, Dwaparayuga, and Kaliyuga. They correspond to the four phases of human life. The number four has significance in weights and measures and as a monetary unit. For example, a kilogram or pound is divided into four equal parts for measuring purposes. A rupee or a dollar is also divided into four quarters. In many countries, the basic unit of currency, such as the dollar or the rupee, is divided into four quarters.

Four stands for perfection, symmetry, and completeness. It symbolizes the earth since the earth has four directions and is complete in itself. At one time, it was believed to rest on four pillars. The land, be it agricultural or residential, is usually divided into squares or rectangles since it is the most convenient way to measure each plot. The four corners of the Earth (chaturanta) signify the vastness or expansiveness of the world we live in. In the days when the Earth was believed to be flat, they denoted the end of the world on all four sides. A crossroads is where four paths or corners meet. Hence, it is often called a public square or convenient place where people from all walks of life and all corners of a city or village meet to discuss, share, or exchange their opinions and goods. The Hebrew name for God

(YHVH) consists of four letters. In Christianity, four signifies the Christian cross since it has four points which denote, maybe God (YHVH), the four corners of the earth, courage, fortitude, suffering, a meeting place where worshippers congregate, and the bridge to heaven. The New Testament has four gospels. The Book of Revelations mentions the Four Horsemen of the Apocalypse, who symbolize the four destroyers of life on earth: conquest, war, famine, and death. In Norse mythology, the number four represents the four dwarves (directions) who uphold the sky.

Four has significance in science, too. In living organisms, the DNA that carries genetic information is made up of four nucleotides: adenine (A), thymine (T), cytosine (C), and guanine (G). Four fundamental physical forces govern every activity in Nature and act upon us constantly, namely gravity, electromagnetism, strong nuclear force, and weak nuclear force. In numerology, four represents foundation, stability, order, reliability, and support. In the game of cards, which relies upon chance, the deck of cards contains four suits (hearts, diamonds, clubs, spades), each with specific values in the order of their importance and symbolic meaning. They signify the four classes of humans, and different emotions, qualities, and aspects of life or human experience. In ancient India, people played a game of dice called Krita (mentioned in Chandogya Upanishad) in which whoever threw the number four, all the bets placed on the lower number went to him.

Four is a universal symbol of strength and might where opposites meet and maintain balance and harmony. In many cultures, kings were traditionally known as the lords of the four corners of the earth. Most evolved jivas are either four-legged or have two hands and two legs, which double or quadruple their strength and agility. Traditionally, kings in ancient India organized their armies into four basic units: infantry consisting of foot soldiers and archers, cavalry, elephants, and chariots. A king who possessed such an army was known as a fourfold mighty king (chaturangabali) for whom the world would surrender. Based on this only, the game of chaturanga (chess) was invented in ancient India for the delight of kings and nobles. Even today, one can see the fourfold division of a modern army consisting of the airborne, infantry, armored, and mountain divisions. According to the U.S. Department of Defense, four soldiers make a team.

Atheistic and rationalistic philosophies identify four elements as the basis of life and existence: earth, water, fire, and air. A triangular pyramid with four equal triangular faces (tetrahedron) had great significance in ancient Egyptian cultures as a resurrection machine, a bridge between this world and the next, and a symbol of authority, majesty, and immortality. In Chinese, Korean, and Japanese cultures, the number four is considered inauspicious since it sounds similar to the word for death in Mandarin. Therefore, like number 13 in Western cultures, the number four is omitted in marking the floors in high-rise buildings in many parts of East Asia. Yet, people in these countries practice Buddhism in which the Four Noble Truths and the Eightfold Path have great significance. In contrast, an Indigenous tribe known as the Zia of New Mexico, USA, regards the number four as auspicious because their ancestors were believed to be from an area known as the Four Corners region in the southwestern USA.

Four is the only number in English with the same number of letters as its value. In Sanskrit, four is known as Chatur, which, grammatically, is always used as a plural. Like the previous three numbers, its base form also changes with each case and gender, as shown below.

Vibhakti (Case)	Pullingam (Masculine)	Streelingam (Feminine)	Napunsaklingam (Neuter)
Prathama	Chatvarah	Chatasrah	Chatvari
Dvitiya	Chaturah	Chatasrah	Chatvari
Tritiya	Chatubhih	Chatsrubhih	Chaturbhih
Chaturthi	Chatubhyah	Chatasrubhya	Chatubhya
Panchami	Chatubhya	Chatasrubhya	Chatubhya
Shashti	Chaturnaam	Chatasrunaam	Chaturnaam
Saptami	Chatursu	Chatasrursu	Chatursu

In Hinduism, four represents divinity, power, strength, balance, unity, harmony, and symmetry. It has great symbolic, geometric, social, and ritual significance. In Meghadutam, Kalidasa describes Mount Kailash as standing magnificently with four peaks (chatvari sringa) and a strong triangular base (trayogasya pada), denoting its stability, divinity, and majesty. The Brihadaranyaka Upanishad describes Brahman as a four-legged horse since He is the lord of space, who rules the earth and the heaven in four directions, can move swiftly through space as sound in any direction, and connects people and places, and gods and humans to facilitate the progression of life. The Chandogya Upanishad (3.12.6) declares that the mortal world with all the beings in it constitutes his one foot. The rest are in heaven. It also states (3.18.2) how, in four ways, a human being (Purusha) extends his reach: by speech, by vital energy, by sight, and by ear,

Brahma is known as a god with four faces (Chaturaanan). They denote his omniscience and control over all knowledge and intelligence. Brihadaranyaka Upanishad (5.14.1) describes the Gayatri meter as having four feet, with the sun (Brahman) in the high skies acting as its fourth foot. That foot also rests on Truth. The Upanishad (5.8.1) also states that one should meditate on speech as a cow with four teats: the sound Svaha, the sound Vasat, the sound Hanta, and the sound Svadha, which are uttered while offering oblations to the gods. Chandogya Upanishad (3.12.5) also states that Gayatri has four feet and six forms.

The Vedas divide a human being's life into four phases. The first phase is known as Brahmacharya, which is the period of celibacy and study under a teacher who should be respected and followed as if he is a personification of Brahma (gururbrahma). The second phase is known as Grihasta, during which the young adult, after completing his education, should begin his life as a householder and engage in obligatory duties according to his nature or caste. The third phase is known as Vanaprastha, during which the householder should withdraw from active duties and go to a secluded place, such as a forest, and live there in solitude like a hermit, practicing contemplation and spiritual transformation. The fourth and final phase is known as Sannyasa, during which one should renounce all desires and attachments and live like an ascetic, working for his liberation. These four phases also correspond to the four parts of a day: the morning, afternoon, evening, and night.

Four also figures prominently in the social and religious lives of Hindus. In the past, society was divided into four Varnas. The Vedas are four in number: Rigveda, Samaveda, Yajurveda, and Atharvaveda.

Each of them is further divided into four parts: Samhita, Brahmanas, Aranyakas, and Upanishads. They declare four chief aims of life that humans must pursue while upholding and performing God's eternal duties: Dharma, Artha, Kama, and Moksha. Many Hindus pray to God or make offerings, turning around in four directions. They circumambulate around temples, which are built in rectangular or square shapes. Indeed, squares are inherent to the basic design and layout of many Hindu temples. The entrance hall (artha-mandapa), the main open hall (mandapa), and the sanctum (garbhagudi) of many temples are built according to the geometric shape of a square. Some temples may have more than one mandapa (open halls), and they are also laid out in the same manner. A square represents the world itself. Each corner and the midpoint between two corners represent the eight directions of the earth, each ruled by a deity. The space within each square in a temple is also divided into smaller squares and rectangles, each representing an important Vedic deity. Many sacrificial altars for performing the fire sacrifices are built in square shapes. Houses, royal buildings, and public structures in the past were built using squares as the basic layout.

In the macrocosm, four represents Dharma. It is the fourth principle, entity, power, or divinity to manifest in creation, after Purusha, Prakriti, and the Field of Prakriti or the material universe (Viraj). Hindu scriptures depict Dharma as a goddess with four legs. When she walks on four legs, truth, peace, harmony, virtue, Rta, and righteousness prevail. In each of the four great yugas, she gradually loses one leg, resulting in the gradual ascendence of evil, disorder, chaos, and the final destruction of all. Kamadhenu, the sacred cow and giver of boons, is also depicted in the imagery as a four-legged deity.

While Rta (or Rtam) enforces the natural orderliness of creation, it is not effective in ensuring the order and regularity of everything that exists in creation. It is especially ineffective against humans or intelligent creatures since they engage in willful actions according to their desires and attachments or their essential nature (svabhavam). Since they are deluded and ignorant, they can potentially disrupt the progression of the world and their liberation by pursuing egoistic desires and attachments and engaging in sinful actions. By their ignorant actions, they may not only bring ruin upon themselves due to the influence of Maya but also disrupt the world and create chaotic conditions unless they are controlled by established norms, laws, and regulations and made to face the consequences of their actions and learn from their suffering. Dharma fulfills that purpose. It presents them with a superior system of values, obligations, divine laws, duties, and moral percepts by which they can avoid sinful conduct, live righteously, perform their duties, and fulfill their obligations to God as His instruments. By living righteously, serving God, following the moral precepts ordained by the scriptures, cultivating purity and equanimity, and performing obligatory duties selflessly as a sacrifice, they can also attain peace and happiness and qualify for liberation, which is the ultimate aim the human life on Earth.

Thus, Dharma becomes the fourth most important aspect in the general scheme of creation. Like a square or rectangle, it acts like an enclosure, protecting those who remain within the limits or the boundaries it sets for the people on Earth. Those who practice Dharma and live their lives righteously with exemplary conduct are protected by its presiding deity. As the adage goes, "Those who protect and uphold Dharma are protected and upheld by Dharma." Dharma is a system of religious and moral laws introduced by Brahman to the mortal world through the Vedas to assist humans in their journey on earth. Its aim is twofold: to preserve Rta, the divine order and regularity of the world, and to help humans achieve their four chief aims, namely Dharma, Artha, Kama, and Moksha, by performing their duties and fulfilling their obligations to God.

Thus, Dharma, the number four in creation, helps humans achieve the fourth chief aim (Moksha) and attain the fourth world, the immortal world of Brahman. All the divinities that manifest in creation are meant to uphold Dharma. Most of the Hindu gods and goddesses possess four hands, which can be seen in their images. Those four hands give them the strength and power required to enforce Dharma, the fourth power to manifest in creation. The divinities we know in Hinduism are but a small percentage of a vast multitude of gods operating in higher planes and are largely unknown. Some of them descend into our plane for a brief period for a specific purpose and then withdraw forever, leaving behind a brief reference in a long lineage of gurus and schools of thought.

Dharma is eternal (Sanatana) because, whatever the time and space may be, it will always be the same. It is manifested at the beginning of creation and withdrawn at the end. Because it is not created, we always receive it as bits and pieces of revelation. What is revealed is only a part of the much greater Dharma, and no one knows its full extent except Brahman himself. It is revealed by the divine intent to help the beings and guide them on the righteous path. Most importantly, it can be revealed only to those who are qualified to receive it by virtue of their knowledge and their inner purity. Dharma declines from time to time to the extent that beings move out of their paths and disturb the Rtam. Whenever there is disorder and decline of Dharma, Vishnu reincarnates as a mortal being upon the earth and restores order.

The number four is thus a symbolic representation of the eternal Dharma, which is the traditional name for Hinduism. It is the solution to the problem of ahamkara or ego, the fourth in the 24 tattvas (principles) of creation. Dharma, the corpus of moral, religious, and spiritual duties which forms a part of the Divine Law, has four legs. In each Maha yuga or epoch, it progressively loses one leg. Thus, in the first epoch, Dharma walks on four legs, in the second on three, in the third on two, and in the last, which is the current epoch, on only one. The world will end when the fourth leg is completely lost. The Vedas, which constitute the Dharma, are also four in number. The Vedas are eternal. Brahma revealed them to his mind-born sons. Lord Vishnu is their protector and preserver. And Lord Siva helps us to understand them by destroying our ignorance.

In Hinduism, the number four is also associated with many other concepts, some of which we have already discussed.

- The four chief aims of human life: According to the Vedas, householders and karma yogis must pursue four chief aims (purusharthas) in their lives, namely Dharma (righteousness), Artha (wealth), Kama (desire), and Moksha (salvation).
- The four Ashramas of Vedic Dharma: The Vedas identify four stages (ashramas) of human life: Brahmacharya (life as a celibate student, Grihasta (life as a householder), Vanaprastha (life as a hermit following retirement and withdrawal from

obligatory duties), and Sannyasa (life as an ascetic in the pursuit of liberation). However, everyone doesn't need to follow them in the same order. One may enter a life of renunciation at any time if one wishes to.
- The four classes of humans: The ancient Vedic Varna System classified humans into four major classes based on their birth: Brahmanas, Kshatriyas, Vaisyas, and Sudras. According to the Vedas, they were born from different parts of Purusha, the Cosmic Being, during a sacrificial ritual. The Varnas determined the duties of each person at the time of birth. Gradually, the system morphed into the present social system with numerous caste groups that have little resemblance to the ancient Varnas or the system that perpetuated the disparities.
- The four Vedas: The Vedas are four: Rigveda, Samaveda, Yajurveda, and Atharvaveda. Just as the number four, the four Vedas denote completeness, perfection, divine authority, and inviolability. Their word is believed to be final in all matters. They represent the four divine feet of the all-pervading Universal Brahman, who is often compared to a celestial horse. A Brahmana who has knowledge or mastery of the four Vedas is called Chaturvedi. He is not only knowledgeable of the four Vedas but also wise and skillful (chatura) in using that knowledge.
- The four divisions of an army: In ancient India, a king's army was divided into four main divisions: infantry, cavalry, chariots, and elephantry. The last one was subsequently replaced by artillery. This structure subsequently gave birth to the game of chess (chaturanga or chadaranga). The four divisions exemplify the symbolism of the number four, denoting strength, unity, harmony, balance, intelligence, and fortitude.
- Chaturvidhopaya: Indian tradition prescribes four conventional methods or approaches (upayas) for resolving conflicts, enmity, or rivalry between rulers or opposing parties, namely Sama (cultivating friendship), Dana (giving financial assistance), Bheda (dividing and creating internal divisions), and Danda (using the stick).

- Connection with time: A day, month, or year, or the lifetime of a person on earth, can be divided into four equal parts. A great epoch has four epochs. In the Hindu calendar, Shravana, Bhadrapada, Ashwin, and Kartika constitute the four-month period known as Chaturmas during which important Hindu festivals are celebrated, including Maha Shivaratri, Ganesh Chaturthi, Navaratri, and Diwali. It is also the period during which Lord Vishnu is believed to enter yogic sleep (Yoganidra), resting on his serpent, Adishesha.
- Significance in astrology: Chaturdamsha, commonly known as D4, refers to the fourth of the sixteen supplemental divisional charts in Vedic astrology, which reveals a person's fortune (bhagya), health, wealth, wellbeing, happiness, prosperity, and other aspects based on the planetary positions and the ascendant sign at the time of that person's birth.
- Connection with knowledge and wisdom: In certain aspects, four signifies knowledge and intelligence. In Sanskrit, chatur means not only four but also "intelligent" or "smart." This second meaning probably gained significance to denote someone proficient in the four Vedas, possessed four distinct types of knowledge, cleverly resolved problems, or performed actions with distinct skills.
- Affinity with water: Of the five elements (mahabhuta), water is the fourth element to manifest in creation. The order of their manifestation is space, fire, air, water, and earth. Most likely, life must have also manifested on Earth in the same way, first in space, then in fire, air, water, and earth successively. The water element, the fourth in the order, is grosser than space, fire, and air but subtler than the earth element. It has great significance in Hindu rituals and spiritual practices and is used for ritual bathing, sanctifying the images, rituals, and ritual places, and making daily offerings.
- Similarity with consciousness: The number four has a deep connection with consciousness. Both are represented by the water element and share its fluidity and plasticity. Consciousness has four states: wakeful, dream, deep sleep, and transcendental, and has four aspects: thoughts, perceptions, feelings,

and concepts or ideas, which are used for controlling the mind in concentration, meditation, and mindfulness practices.
- Symbolic connection with divinity: The number four represents many divine qualities, such as balance, harmony, completeness, inclusiveness, omniscience, diversity, and stability. Brahma is known as Chaturaanan or Chaturmukha since he has four faces, which denote his all-knowing awareness. Brahman has four highest aspects: the absolute, indescribable, pure and undifferentiated state (Brahman), the Cosmic germ or Self (Hiranyagarbha), the self-luminous Supreme Being, Cosmic Mind or God (Isvara), and the Cosmic Body or the material universe (Viraj) illuminated by and filled with the presence of the other three. Many Hindu gods and goddesses are depicted in the images as having four hands. They denote their indomitable power, superior strength, universal reach, and other divine attributes.
- Symbolic correspondence with space: The number four is comparable to space and represents its expansiveness, vastness, inclusiveness, complexity, diversity, and dimensions: length, width, height, or depth, and time. Just as space with its four dimensions, mathematically and geometrically, four can accommodate complex shapes, forms, and structures like the tesseract, a 4D analogue of a cube [1]. The symbolic connection between space and number four is further affirmed by the fact that the Earth has four quarters and eight directions, each ruled by a Vedic deity who acts as its guardian.
- As a source of diversity: Like Nature, four represents diversity, which is well reflected in many objects in Nature, such as certain crystal structures and tiling patterns, and in many mathematical and physical systems that contain fourfold rotational symmetry. A rectangle or square can accommodate numerous equal or unequal triangles, comparable to the finite realities and diversity arising from Prakriti. The four-sided polygon (quadrilateral) represents geometric diversity and can accommodate many forms and shapes: squares, rectangles, trapezoids, parallelograms—each with distinct characteristics.

References

1. Wikipedia, Four-dimensional space

Five Panchan

In many cultures, the number five represents unity, strength, brotherhood, status, authority, seniority, and the elemental world, which is made up of the five elements. In ancient India, and even now in some remote areas, villages were governed by an informal committee of five elders known as the panchas. The chief of such committees was known as Sarpanch, meaning the head of the panchas and the system that governed their activities as the panchayat. The government of India still uses this nomenclature to designate the village leaders elected by the people and the local committees they represent. In the past, the panchas settled local disputes and prescribed punishments and remedies. In extreme cases, they had the authority to excommunicate or permanently expel people from their villages for serious crimes or violations of social norms. Hinduism also recognizes five chief virtues and five chief evils. The decision, opinion, or evidence of five people was accepted without question. Since the senses are also five, it lent legitimacy to this practice. Thus, five symbolized the weight of law and authority in the social and secular matters of Hindus until a century ago. The ancient system may still exist in some remote parts of India.

In mathematics, the number five is a prime number and a Fibonacci number (0, 1, 1, 2, 3, 5) [1]. It is the first digit formed by the sum of the first odd (3) and the first even (2) numbers. Geometrically, it can be depicted as a pentagon, a pentagram, a five-pointed star polygon, or simply a five-pointed polygram. The pentagram has mystic significance in various traditions and cultures. The Greeks regarded it as a symbol of light, health, and vitality. The five-pointed star is a widely recognized symbol that appears in many national and institutional flags, including the US flag. The five extensions of the start symbolize the five elements, five ways of something, apart from shining qualities, such as achievement, excellence, bravery, wealth, power, fame, or stardom. The phrase "five-star" is frequently used to denote excellence in quality, service, value, etc. The Egyptians used a five-pointed star in their hieroglyphs. For the Greeks, it symbolized Venus. In Christianity, it symbolizes the birth and the five wounds of Christ, while in Hinduism, it represents the north star (Dhruva tara) or any bright star.

Many religious traditions and cultures identify five virtues, morals, practices, restraints, and laws to govern human conduct or enforce discipline. The reasons may be that it is convenient and easier to memorize and remember. Five serves as a reasonable and practical standard that is neither too many nor too few. Pythagoras considered the number five a symbol of Nature, representing balance and equilibrium, since it divides the perfect number ten into two equal parts (10/2=5). Besides, it represented ether, the fifth element in his estimate, which is impervious to the actions of Nature and is unaffected by the remaining four elements it contains. Pythagoras also saw five as a unique number that reproduces itself when it is multiplied by itself (5x5=25), just as life reproduces itself in Nature. He called it the Pentad, which the Greeks regarded as a symbol of reconciliation, alternation, marriage, immortality, cordiality, providence, and sound. They also perceived it as a symbol of divinity since they found similar qualities in several Greek deities such as Pallas, Nemesis, Bubastia (Bast), Venus, Androgynia, and others.

In Sanskrit, the number five, known as pancha, is always used grammatically as a plural. Its basic form may vary according to each case, but its form remains the same for the three genders as shown below. This rule applies to all the numbers from 5-18. They are all used in the plural for all seven cases. For numbers 19 onwards, their forms are always in the singular. This is because Sanskrit treats numbers 5–18 as adjectives that can be used to qualify plural nouns, while numbers 19 and beyond are treated as abstract numerical concepts.

Vibhakti	Male	Female	Neuter
Prathamaa	Pancha	Pancha	Pancha
Dvitiyaa	Pancha	Pancha	Pancha
Tritiyaa	Panchabhih	Panchabhih	Panchabhih
Chaturthi	Panchabhyah	Panchabhyah	Panchabhyah
Panchami	Pacha:	Pacha:	Pacha:
Shasthi	Panchanaam	Panchanaam	Panchanaam
Saptami	Pachasu	Pachasu	Pachasu

In Hinduism, five symbolizes the gross physical body (annamaya kosa), the earth element, and the planet Earth. Visually, it represents the overall physical appearance of a human being with five visible parts: two hands, two legs, and one head. When outstretched, they mirror the five points of a pentagram. The gross physical body is made up of five elements: space, air, fire, water, and earth. The earth element was the fifth in the order in which the elements appeared in creation. Space or ether (Akasa) is the first element, the essence of God himself. Omnipresent, it has always existed and was never created. None of the senses can reach it, including the mind, but it acts as the medium of sounds, accommodates and facilitates the whole existence, and supports all perceptions. Air (Vayu) is next. It is subtle and closer to space in some respects, but is still within the reach of the mind through touch, inference, and feeling. Agni (fire) is the third element, also subtle and similar to Vayu in some respects, but perceptible through form (flames), color, heat, sound, and smell. Both Vayu and Agni belong to the mid-region (Bhur), while the Akasa (space) element belongs to the higher region (Suva). Water (jalam), the fourth element, is the most important of all since life on Earth depends upon it. Earth is the fifth element. It is the densest and the grossest of the five. Our bodies are made up of these five, but of them, the earth and water elements are the most predominant.

Our earthly bodies are mostly composed of the last two elements, the densest of the five. Hence, we are limited in our movements, awareness, and experience. The physical body is called Annamaya Kosa because it is created mostly by the food (annam) we eat. This food, in turn, is produced from the earth. Hence, in a way, it is also the earth body. It is the outermost sheath of our bodies and depends exclusively upon food and other gross and subtle objects for nourishment, enjoyment, and contact with the outside world. Because we are subject to duality and the fact that our bodies are the most visible proof of our existence, and our personalities and consciousness, we identify with them and consider them to be the defining aspects of ourselves. As long as we are attached to this identity, we remain bound, ignorant, and deluded. Ascetics who realize this withdraw their minds and senses inwardly and detach themselves from their physical identities. They practice austerities and spiritual discipline and transcend their dependence on and attachment to their bodies. Through self-control and self-purification, they transcend the gunas and reach a stage where they can survive without food for extended periods and remain absorbed within themselves. Some believe that either God helps them or they learn to nourish themselves through other means, such as drawing prana (vital energy) into their nadis (nerve channels) from outside.

The earth-body, which corresponds to the five points of a pentagram and is made up of five elements, remains connected to the world of five elements and receives its nourishment and enjoyment through the five senses, namely the skin, eyes, nose, ears, and tongue. They help the jivas by facilitating five ways of knowing, being, and perceiving. We, as humans, with all our senses, mind, and intelligence fully developed, rely upon them to interact with the objects of our world and ensure our survival and wellbeing. Corresponding to the five senses (jnanedriyas) are the five organs of action (karmendriyas), namely the hands, legs, reproductive organs, larynx, and anus. They perform the five bodily functions of grasping, walking, generating, speaking, and emitting. They are the five ways in which these organs function and support our existence. In addition to them, there are five subtle or internal senses known as tanmatras, namely touching, seeing, smelling, hearing, and tasting. They represent the five ways in which we connect to the world and experience reality.

Human beings have all the external and internal sense organs, but subtle beings (gods, gandharvas, yakshas, and the like) will have only subtle senses or tanmatras, which means they can experience reality and grasp knowledge without relying upon physical senses or the mind. Hindu scriptures suggest that those who engage in spiritual and ascetic practices such as yoga and tantra persistently can awaken their subtle senses and attain extraordinary siddhis or supernatural powers, with which they can experience the world differently, even when their senses are withdrawn or inactive. Regardless of the truth, indeed, the number five symbolically represents the earth and the physical body. It is hidden in the basic structure and function of our bodies and this world. In each human body (the village), the panchas (aggregates of five) perform their obligatory duties (Dharma) at various levels, controlling and ensuring its functions, order and regularity, while the person (sarpanch) within acts as the head or lord, ensuring the wellbeing of all.

However, this is not the only symbolism associated with the number five. In Hinduism, the number has even greater significance and is associated with many other important concepts, beliefs, and practices, some of which are briefly mentioned below.

- Five divine manifestations: According to Shaivism, the Supreme Lord, Parama Shiva or Parameswara, has five supreme manifestations: Brahma (creator), Vishnu (preserver), Rudra (destroyer), Maheswara (concealer), and Sadashiva (revealer). Hence, Shiva is known as Panchanan Shiva, the fivefold Shiva or Shiva with five faces. In Vaishnavism, as the Lord of the Universe, Narayana or Lord Vishnu has five supreme aspects: Para (transcendent), Vyuha (emanating), Vibhava (incarnating), Antaryami (immanent), and Arcavatara (consecrated images worshipped in temples). In Vedism, Brahman has five supreme manifestations: Brahman, Isvara, Hiranyagarbha, Viraj, and Time or Death.
- Five supreme qualities: Vedanta refers to the five divine qualities of Isvara, the Supreme Being, or Saguna Brahman: Truth (satyam), Knowledge (jnanam), Infinity (anantam), Bliss (anandam), and Purity (amalatvam). Those who attain liberation also possess them.
- Five fires: The Vedas mention five sacred fires, Anvaharya or Dakshina, Garhapatya, Avahaniya, Sabhya, and Avasthya. In olden days, higher castes, especially Brahmanas, were ordained to maintain these fires in their homes to perform daily and occasional sacrifices to nourish the gods and others as a part of their householder Dharma.
- Five types of devotion: Vaishnava literature mentions five types of devotion: Samanya (ordinary), Sadhana (with practice), Bhava (with emotions), Prema (with love), and Uttama (with purity) [2].
- Five devotional services: In traditional forms of worship, devotees offer five types of devotional services to the gods, corresponding to the five elements and five sense organs (fan, water, flame, incense, and food).
- Five limbs of Vedic astrology: In Sanskrit, the Hindu calendar is called Panchangam since it contains five factors (angas) used

by Hindu astrologers (jyotishyas) to determine auspicious and inauspicious times, namely Tithi (date or position of the sun), Vaara (day of the week), Nakshatra (position of the stars), Karana (position of the moon), and Yoga (lunar conjunction). They are also known as panchashuddhi since they cleanse and neutralize the five negative influences of Time (Kala), also known as Death.

- The Self as a river of five streams: The Svetasvatara Upanishad (1.4) states that one should meditate upon Brahman, the divine Self (divyatma), as a river of five streams (consciousness), having five fierce and crooked sources, whose waves are the five breaths, whose root cause is the five types of intelligence, and which contain five whirlpools and five fast flowing pains divided into five branches and fifty kinds of suffering. Each of these groups of five refers to various aspects of the mind and its modifications.

- Panchamritam: In Hindu temples, worshippers offer the deities a special preparation called Panchamritam made from five sweet ingredients: curd, honey, sugar, fresh (cow) milk, and ghee. It is considered very sacred and pleasing to the deities and beneficial to the devotees, with healing and medicinal properties.

- Five arrows of sensual passion: The human mind is susceptible to five human passions, each corresponding to a particular sense. Manmadha, the god of love, is known as Pancheshu and Panchasara because he wields five arrows, which represent these five passions. With them, he pierces the hearts of lovers and deludes them. The arrows are made from specific flowers: the white lotus, the red flower, the mango blossom, the fresh jasmine, and the blue water lily, symbolizing the progressive stages of falling in love and evoking five specific passions through the five senses. They represent the desire for pleasure, deep attraction, infatuation or delusion, emotional vulnerability, and death or complete loss of self-control, respectively.

- Fifth state: When a person is alive, he is subject to four states of consciousness, wakeful, dream, deep sleep, and transcendental states. When he dies, consciousness ceases to exist in the body, and with that, the four states also. Further, when a person is alive, all five elements in the body are active. Upon death, the four elements present in the body resolve into their elemental state as soon as the body is cremated, leaving the fifth element, space or akasa, intact for some time. Death, therefore, is the fifth state (panchama avastha). Hence, when a person dies, he is said to be in the fifth state.

- Panchavayava: The Nyaya School of Hinduism recognizes five components of a logical argument or syllogism known as panchavayava to construct valid arguments or establish reasonable truths, namely, pratijna (proposition), hetu (reason), udaharana (example), upanaya (application), and nigamana (conclusion). They are used in Nyaya and Vaishesika schools to arrive at the right knowledge or right understanding, or overcome ignorance and incorrect knowledge and understanding. They are also used in Ayurveda to establish scientific truths or principles.

- Panchagupt: Withdrawing the senses into the mind has been one of the established practices for meditation and contemplation. For a long time, the tortoise has been used as a prime metaphor for this practice. The tortoise is known as panchagupt because it tends to withdraw its limbs into the shell and keeps them hidden or private (gupt) to protect itself or rest. The philosophy of the atheists of ancient India, known as Charvakas, was also known by this name, probably because they kept the five main practices or principles of their teachings a secret.

- Five digestive fires: Vedic scriptures mention five digestive fires (energies) that assist in the digestion, transformation, and assimilation of food in the body and keep the body nourished and alive. When people renounce worldly life and take the vows of sannyasa, they aim to keep these fires alive by generating bodily heat (tapa) through austerity and conservation of energy, while renouncing the use of external fires for any purpose. The five digestive fires that keep working in the body are Jatharagni (the central digestive fire in the intestines), Bhutagni (the five elemental fires corresponding to the five elements that help assimilate elemental energies in food), Dhatwagni (the seven fires, one for each tissue in the body, namely rasa, rakta, mamsa, meda, asthi, majja, and shukra). Pachakagni (a subset of jatharagni that governs the enzymatic and metabolic processes), and Ranjakagni (found in the liver and spleen, which aids in the production and metabolism of blood). These five are said to be aspects of Agni, or more particularly, the Vaisvanara fire, often described in the Upanishads as universal consciousness

- Panchakarma: Ayurveda has an important concept called panchakarma, which describes five primary methods for treating illnesses and bodily impurities: vamana (therapeutic emesis, which involves controlled vomiting), virechana (therapeutic purgation, in which herbal laxatives are used to cleanse the gastrointestinal tract and eliminate excess pitta dosha), basti (enema therapy, in which medicated oils or herbal decoctions are administered through the rectum to cleanse the colon), nasya (nasal administration which involves the use of medicated oils or powders through the nasal passages to clear toxins from the head and neck region), and raktamokshana (bloodletting, which involves the controlled removal of impure blood to treat conditions caused by blood-borne toxins, such as skin disorders and certain inflammatory conditions).
- Five cow products: Cows are sacred in Hinduism. Even in the days when animal sacrifices were popular and not considered taboo, cows were never used for sacrifice. Instead, it has been customary for a long time to give cows as gifts to Brahmanas and use five cow products in Vedic sacrifices and domestic rituals as purifiers. They are milk, curds, clarified butter, ghee, and urine.
- Five classes of beings: According to the Puranas, when Brahma began creation, he created five classes of beings: devas (gods), asuras (demons), manavas (humans), pashus (animals), and rakshasas. They denote the diversity of creation.
- Five tantric substances: In some schools of Tantra, five substances, wine, meat, fish, mudra (gesture), and intercourse, are used in rituals to gain control over the mind and body and attain liberation or supernatural powers. These rituals constitute

unconventional left-hand methods or practices (vamachara), in contrast to the traditional, right-hand methods of Hinduism known as Vedachara.

- Panchapranas: In some ancient texts, the senses are often equated with the breaths (pranas), probably because vital energy (prana) flows through them into the body. Some Upanishads refer to five vital energies known as Panchapranas that flow in the body, namely Prana, Apana, Vyana, Udana, and Samana. They are distinguished by their location, function, and flow in the body. When a person dies, they depart from the body and join their counterparts in the macrocosm.
- Pancha mahapatakas: Hindu scriptures mention five mortal sins, or gravest depravities known as pancha mahapatakas, which disrupt the order and regularity of the world and lead to serious repercussions. They are brahmahatya (killing a brahmana or a spiritual person), surapana (consuming alcoholic or intoxicating substances), steya (stealing or unlawfully taking what does not belong to oneself), gurvanga-gamana (engaging in an inappropriate relationship with the spouse of a teacher or guru), and mahapataka (helping or associating with those who commit these mortal sins). According to the Garuda Purana, those who engage in them receive the harshest punishments in hell.
- Five daily sacrifices: According to the Vedic tradition, Hindu householders must perform five daily sacrifices (nitya karmas) to uphold God's eternal duties (Dharma) and ensure the welfare of the family and order and regularity of the world. The five daily sacrifices are brahma yajna, offering food to seers, sages, and the worshippers of Brahman; deva yajna, offering food to the gods in heaven; pitru yajna, offering food to the ancestors awaiting their rebirth in the ancestral world; bhuta yajna, offering food to all living beings; and manushya yajna, offering food to fellow humans who are in need. Those who perform them are ensured a minimum good life in their next birth because of their good karma.
- Five distinguishing features of the Puranas: Hinduism has a vast body of literature. Of them, the Puranas are important.

They are distinguished by five main features, topics, or characteristics, known as panchalakshanas. They are, sarga (accounts of creation describing how the worlds and beings came into existence), pratisarga (accounts of secondary creation narrating the cycles of destruction and recreation), vamsha (genealogies recounting the histories of the lineages and the greatness of gods, sages, and illustrious kings), manvantara (descriptions of cosmic ages detailing the accounts of the reigns of Manus, progenitors of human races in each cosmic age), and vamshanucharita (family histories recollecting the myths, legends and histories of royal dynasties, kings, and their deeds).

- Five types of salts: Salt carries great importance in Ayurveda and Hindu alchemy (rasashastra). These ancient sciences prescribe five types of salts for medicinal or health purposes: saindhava lavana, rock salt, known for its cooling properties and digestive benefits; samudra lavana, sea salt, commonly used in cooking and rituals; sauvarchala lavana, black salt, recognized for its flavor and digestive properties; vida lavana, a type of salt used in traditional medicine for its therapeutic value; and sambara lavana, a lesser-known salt used in specific medicinal preparations.
- Panchavata: Ayurveda identifies five types of airs (vata) that govern communication and movements in the body, named after the five pranas (vital energies) that flow in the body. They are Prana, Vyana, Udana, Samana, and Apana. Disturbances in them lead to their irregular flow in the body (Vata Dosha).
- Pancha Pandavas: The number five signifies unity, strength, brotherhood, and diversity of Nature, which is well reflected in the Pandavas of the epic Mahabharata. They had a divine connection, each being born from a god, besides sharing the same nature (symbolized by Draupadi), and fighting unitedly against injustice, evil, and unrighteousness (adharma) represented by the Kauravas. The five Pandavas, Dharmaraja, Bhima, Arjuna, Nakula, and Sahadeva symbolize the five pranas, five senses, five virtues, and five perfections. They also exist in us and participate in the internal battles we face every day against our worst thoughts, desires, and impulses.

- Panchakola: Ayurveda recommends five types of spices, known as Panchakola, having medicinal and digestive properties - Pippali (long pepper), Pippalimula (the root of the long pepper), Chavya (java long-pepper or oriental cashew plant), Chitraka (plumbago), and Nagara (dry ginger). They are used for improving digestion, relieving abdominal pain, detoxifying the body, and treating respiratory problems.
- Panchajnana: According to Buddhist texts, the Buddha possessed five types of knowledge, known as pancha jnana, namely the mirror-like wisdom (adarsha-jnana), the wisdom of equality (samata-jnana), discriminating wisdom (pratyaveksha-jnana), the wisdom of accomplishment (krityanushthana-jnana), and the wisdom of the ultimate reality(dharmadhatu-jnana). Those who possess them attain Nirvana and ascend to the Buddha-like nature.
- Pancha prasada: Since the number five represents qualities such as inclusiveness, diversity, unity, symmetry, strength, and perfection, it is often incorporated into the design and layout of several Hindu temples. For example, temples featuring five shrines or pinnacles (pancha prasada), with a central gopuram or sanctum surrounded by four others in four directions, are common, especially in Northern India. The temples at Khajuraho, Konark, Puri, and Varanasi are well-known examples. In a philosophical sense, the five pinnacles symbolize the five forms of divine grace (abhaya) or five types of spiritual gifts, namely wisdom, devotion, peace, prosperity, and liberation.
- Panchasuna: As we have seen above, the number five is commonly used to group things, names, qualities, persons, buildings, etc., into units, classes, or categories. The concept of panchasuna is one such example. It refers to the five common household tools that, according to Manusmriti (3.68), may unintentionally harm other living beings and lead to five types of sin, suffering, and misfortunes. They are Chulli (fireplace), Peshani (grinding stone), Upaskara (broom), Kandani (pestle and mortar), and Udakumbha (water pot). Since they arise from unintentional actions and lead to unintended consequences,

one should atone for them by performing daily sacrifices, fasting, self-purification, etc.

Reference

1. According to Wikipedia, Fibonacci numbers were said to have been first described by Pingala, an Indian poet and mathematician, about 200 BCE.
2. Śrī Bhakti Rrasāmṛta Sindhu, a principal text of Gaudiya Vaishnavism, written by Śrīla Rūpa Gosvāmī (1489–1564), who was a direct disciple of Śrī Caitanya Mahāprabhu.

Six, Shashtan

In the late 1950s and early 1960s, after India became independent, most currency transactions in villages and local grocery stores used to be in Annas. Local merchants sold goods in Sers (0.933 kg) using standard weights that were in circulation then and collected money often in annas since the anna coins were still in circulation. The word anna was derived from the Sanskrit word anna, meaning grains or food. In those days, one anna was equal to six Indian paise, and 16 annas meant one Indian rupee or 16 annas. The actual value of an anna was 6.25 paise, since the value had to be adjusted to the Indian rupee, which consisted of 100 paise, but people did not mind the difference. They knew that the adjustment became necessary since the government introduced the decimal currency system (in 1957), replacing the older anna system that was prevalent during British rule. The six-paise anna system itself was an improvisation under the new government, since, under the British, the anna was originally equal to four paise, and a rupee was equal to 16 annas or 64 paise. This led to a lot of confusion initially, since the British currency system prevailed in some princely States, until they were fully integrated into the newly formed Indian Republic.

This brief introduction is meant to clear the mistaken notion that the six-paise anna was the basis of the Indian currency system until the British left. The number six was never the basis for any currency system in India, either in the remote past or later. The number four was indeed the basis for both currency and weights. The six paise per anna system was an improvisation necessitated by historical circumstances after the introduction of the decimal currency system and nothing more. The transition from the British system to the Indian often led to minor adjustments as people had to transact business in both currencies, and old anna coins were still in circulation, until the decimal system became the universal norm. At best, six-paise anna was a convenient adaptation to fit the outdated annas into the decimalized rupee.

However, counting by dozens has been an ancient practice that still continues not only in India but in various parts of the world. It is certainly a legacy of an ancient counting system known as the duodecimal system or base-12 system, which was prevalent in ancient Mesopotamia, alongside the sexagesimal system or the base-60, which was probably an improvisation of the duodecimal system. The Babylonians, Egyptians, Greeks, and probably other cultures followed the sexagesimal system for mathematical and astronomical calculations and, maybe, in construction and tool making. Remnants of these ancient methods can still be seen in our regular usage of dozens for counting items and measuring time in seconds, minutes, hours, days, and months. Measuring angles in 360 degrees may also be a remnant of these ancient systems only. In these systems, six is the highest digit by which the numbers 12 and 60 can be divided. Yet, the number 6 was not their basis, and the base-6 number system was not their source. In these cultures, the number six may have had some mystic, mathematical, or symbolic significance, but we cannot be certain.

A counting system based on six, known as Senary or base-6, prevailed in some Babylonian and Sumerian cultures in the past but was never a popular system. The Senary number system had six digits. 0, 1, 2, 3, 4, and 5. The number 6 existed in the base-6 system, not as a digit but as the base number, just as 10 in the decimal system. It carried a different value and was represented differently than in the decimal system. The Senary system had some advantages, as it facilitated better divisions and efficient calculations, but lacked the depth and complexity of the decimal system. Some modern mathematicians and researchers still believe that it has certain advantages and is a better alternative to the binary and decimal systems. In ancient times, the system probably originated from the practice of counting by fingers, and six probably symbolized a full hand.

Mathematically, number six is the smallest perfect number - that is, it is equal to the sum of its proper divisors excluding itself (1,2,3). It is also the highest composite number since it has more divisors (1,2,3, and 6) than any smaller positive integers. Geometrically, six represents a hexagon or a six-sided polygon. Hexagons are found naturally in honeycombs, snowflakes, benzene molecules, certain crystalline structures like graphene, and the north pole of Saturn. In both

Islam and Christianity, the number six has some significance. For example, according to the Bible, God completed creation in six days and created man on the sixth day. Christian ethics stipulate that humans should work six days a week and rest on Sunday, just as God did at the time of creation. Hence, the number also signifies the struggle and suffering that humans endure before they rest six feet under and await their resurrection. Islam holds that God created the world in six days, and the faithful must practice the six articles of faith: belief in Allah, angels, holy books, prophets, the Day of Judgment, and divine decree (qadar). In worldly life, six conveys above-average performance, crossing a threshold, or achieving a landmark, if five is the halfway mark or cutoff point. It also symbolizes balance, order, harmony, perfection, cohesion, unity, and symmetry, aptly represented by the hexagon.

Some of these beliefs and representations were drawn from the symbolism of the ancient Pythagorean schools and other Greek philosophers and later reflected in the teachings of early Christian theologians, such as Clement of Alexandria. In the Pythagorean teachings, the number six (hexad) represented perfection and completeness. These beliefs were also reflected in the depiction or descriptions of Orpheus, Lachesis (one of the Fates), and Thalia (the Muse of comedy and idyllic poetry) of Greek mythology. They regarded the number six (hexad) as a symbol of sacredness and the "maker of the soul." Orpheus, renowned for his music and poetry, saw the hexad as the "form of forms" and the "articulation of the universe," representing the interconnectedness of all things and the association between the Cosmos and the soul. For Lachesis, the hexad embodied "equilibrium," "the cyclical nature of existence," and the "balance between opposites, such as life and death." Thalia, the Muse of comedy and idyllic poetry, saw it as a symbol of creativity and the union of opposites, such as joy and sorrow.

In Hinduism, the number six (sat) has deep symbolic significance and is associated with many important concepts. It represents growth, prosperity, totality, or completeness, etc. Some Sanskrit words and practices of Hinduism allude to the possibility that Vedic people or ancient people of India followed the base-12, base-60, or base-6 numeral system. For example, Hindu householders celebrate

Shastipurthi or Shashtiabdapoorthi at the completion of 60 years of age. The Hindu Saka Era, also known as the Shaka Era, is based on a 60-year cycle. It is very likely that the word shadabdi originally denoted 60 years or the completion of a sixty-year cycle before the decimal system became the norm for measuring time in centuries (satabdi). The Hindu (Vedic) calendar recognizes six seasons: Vasanta (spring), Grishma (summer), Varsha (monsoon), Sharad (autumn), Hemanta (pre-winter), and Shishira (winter). Over the centuries, Indian agricultural and cultural practices, and the celebration of festivals, social and cultural events, evolved based on this sixfold seasonal cycle. Hinduism also recognizes six Darshanas (philosophies), six Vedangas, six Tantras, six rasas (tastes), six chakras, six virtues, and six paths to liberation. Worshipping the deities with the six limbs of the body, known as shashtanga namaskar, is a very popular Hindu practice.

The number 108, which is considered very sacred to Hindus, is divisible by six and gives the resulting number 18, which is also sacred. For example, the Mahabharata has 18 Parvas or sections, the Bhagavadgita has 18 chapters, and the Isa Upanishad has 18 verses. The eight in the 18 represents Goddess Lakshmi, and one represents Lord Vishnu. Alternatively, they represent one Purusha and the eight Shaktis or manifestations of Prakriti.

In many ways, the number six symbolically represents the human mind. Hindu scriptures identify the mind as the sixth sense organ with six faculties: reason, emotion, thought, awareness, knowledge, and intelligence. It is vulnerable to six passions that act as its enemies, obstacles, or impurities: lust, anger, greed, pride, delusion, and envy. The human mind, the most powerful organ of the human body, is the seat of our knowledge and ignorance, and the cause of our bondage and liberation. A mind that is out of control or under the control of these six impurities is the cause of our bondage and suffering. A mind that is pure and withdrawn from the senses into itself is ideal for achieving self-realization, the sixth state of self-absorption. The Upanishads repeatedly emphasize the importance of having a pure mind in the realization of Brahman. So does the Bhagavadgita. So declares the Mundaka Upanishad (3.1.9), *"In the beings, the whole mind is pervaded by the five breaths (senses). When purified, it shines with (the effulgence of) the Self (the sixth)."* In the Maitri Upanishad (6.34), we come across the following verses: *"Even when the mind is quiet, false ideas arise, deluded by the objects of the senses. One's very thought is samsara. Therefore, let one keep the mind pure by effort, for what a man thinks, so he becomes. This is the eternal mystery."* Again, in another verse, it says, *"The mind of a person is of two kinds: pure and impure, impure when it is bound to desire, and pure when it is free."* It is impure when it is subject to the activities of the five senses, the five impurities, and the five sets of modifications, and pure when it is completely free from them.

This pure state of mind is attained when one transcends the fifth state (death) through the practice of yoga, self-discipline, control of the senses, devotion, selfless actions, contemplation, and meditation. The Supreme Path to self-realization begins only when the mind and the five senses are still, and the reason (buddhi) becomes seated in silence (Katha Upanishad). Through the mind, a person experiences three states: the wakeful state (jagrata), the dream state (svapna), and the deep sleep state (susupti). Beyond these three states is the pure (turiya) state of Atman, which is *"neither outer consciousness nor inner consciousness, neither semi-consciousness nor sleeping consciousness, neither consciousness nor unconsciousness."* It is experienced only by transcending the physical mind and entering into a state of samadhi, by becoming pure in thought and deed through yoga and spiritual discipline, and under the guidance of a master. So declares the Maitri Upanishad, "When the mind is silent, beyond weakness or non-concentration, it can enter into a world far beyond the mind, which is the highest end." Between the impure mind (5) and the pure consciousness of the Self (7) is the pure and tranquil mind (6), which is free from desires, duality, and delusion, and firmly established in sameness and equanimity.

The number six is also associated with many important concepts and practices of Hinduism, such as the following.

- Six Vedangas: Anga means limbs, which denotes that it is an extension or an integral part of something bigger. The Vedangas, the limbs or auxiliary disciplines of the Vedas, are six, namely Shiksha (Phonetics), Vyakarana (Grammar), Chhandas

(Meter), Nirukta (Etymology), Jyotisha (Astronomy and Astrology), and Kalpa (Rituals). They assist the students in understanding, interpreting, and applying the knowledge of the Vedas.
- Six Darshanas: Hinduism recognizes six schools of Hindu philosophy, known as Darshanas, meaning visions, perspectives, or schools: Samkhya, Yoga, Nyaya, Vaiseshika, Purva Mimansa, and Uttara Mimansa or Vedanta. Except for the last two, the others may have had an independent origin. They symbolize the relative and diverse nature of intellectual knowledge and the fact that human knowledge can depend upon perspectives. One should therefore keep an open mind and examine all aspects to arrive at the truth.
- Six aesthetic principles: Ancient texts such as the Vishnudharmottara Purana and the Kamasutra by Vatsyayana recognize six important principles in creating aesthetically pleasing art forms or paintings like those found at Ajanta and Ellora. They are known as the six limbs (shadanga) of traditional Indian paintings, namely rupa-bheda (distinction of forms), pramanani (proportion), bhava (emotion or expression), lavanya yojanam (aesthetic composition), sadrisyam (resemblance), and varnika-bhanga (color application).
- Six duties of a Brahman: The Hindu law books prescribe six obligatory duties for pious Brahmanas, namely the study of the Vedas (adhyayana), teaching the Vedas (adhyapana), performing sacrifices (yajana), helping others perform sacrifices (yajna-karana), giving charity (dana), and receiving gifts (pratigraha). In times of difficulties and adversity, they are allowed to practice the following vocations, in addition to these duties: teaching and tutoring, performing rituals for others, trading in goods that are not harmful or against Dharma, practicing agriculture, and accepting gifts or charity to sustain themselves and their families.
- Six cleansing techniques: Certain yoga traditions, like Hath Yoga, describe six cleansing techniques known as shadkarma that are designed to purify and energize the mind and body, namely cleansing the digestive tract (dhauti), the colon (basti),

and the nasal passages (neti), massaging the abdomen by rotating the stomach muscles (nauli), engaging in rapid breathing (kapalabhati), and concentrated gazing (trataka) at an object such as a flame for an extended period.
- Six ritual materials: Hindu tradition recognizes six sacred materials derived from cows that are suitable for medicinal and ritual purposes: milk (dugdha), curd (dadhi), ghee (ghrita), urine (mutra), dung (gomaya), and buttermilk (takra).
- Six qualities or virtues: Hindu texts such as the Vishnu Purana and Bhagavadgita recognize the following six qualities or virtues (ṣatgunas) as divine, which personify the divine nature and state of Isvara, the Supreme Being, and are attributed to Him: knowledge (jnana), strength (bala), sovereignty (aishwarya), energy (shakti), valor (virya), and brilliance (teja).
- Validation by six ears: In ancient times, it was customary to accept the conversation or information heard independently by any three individuals or six ears (shadkarma) as valid proof (pramana) for judgments delivered by presiding authorities. This standard also applied to acknowledging the knowledge of the Vedas as scriptural evidence (shabda pramana) at a time when there were no written texts, and the Vedas were only heard and not recorded.
- Shadamnaya: Hindu Tantra contains references to six traditions, six secrets, and six sacred streams of knowledge or teachings, said to have originated from the six faces of Lord Shiva. The concept also refers to the six directions (north, south, east, west, above, and below) inhabited by the omniscient, omnipresent Supreme Lord.
- Shastamsa: In ancient India, a ruler was entitled to one-sixth (shastamsa) of the produce as tax from the farmers who cultivated the lands under his protection.
- Six magical actions: The Atharvaveda, and some tantric texts of the Shakta and Shaiva traditions recognize six actions (shatkarmas) as lawful, which involve mystical and magical rituals and the chanting of esoteric mantras: healing and protection, prosperity and success, love and relationships, exorcism and purification, agricultural blessings, and spiritual enlightenment.

According to another version, the six actions included creating peace (shanti), deluding or subjugating (vasikarana), immobilizing (sthambana), creating enmity (vidvesha), ruining or eradicating an enemy (ucchatana), and causing death (marana).
- Shadja, the sixth musical note: Of the seven Indian primary musical notes (swaras) - Sa, Re, Ga, Ma, Pa, Dha, Ni, the first note (Sa) is known as Shadja because it arises from the six organs of the human body: nose (nasam), throat (kantam), chest (urastha), tongue (jihva), teeth (dantam), and the touch of the tongue (sasprushan). A musical melody or composition that includes six of the seven primary notes is known as shaadava.
- Six types of forts: Kautilya's Artha Shastra recognizes six types of forts (ṣaṭdurga), namely water fort (jal durga), hill fort (giri durga), forest fort (vana durga), desert fort (dhanu durga), earthen or mud fort (mahi durga), and human fort (manushya durga).
- Six types of knowledge: In literary circles, having six types of Vedic knowledge (satprajña) is considered a distinction, namely the knowledge of the four Purusharthas or chief aims of human life (Dharma, Artha, Kama, and Moksha), the knowledge of the nature of the empirical world, and the knowledge of the nature of the Supreme Self.
- Goddesses with six arms: Durga is known as Ṣaṭbhuja because she is depicted in the imagery with six arms, each holding a specific weapon signifying her power and might against forces of evil. Hence, in mystic diagrams like the Durga Yantra, she is symbolically represented as a hexagon(ṣaṭkona). Other goddesses with six arms are Vasudhara and Mahaguari. The arms also symbolize her diversity, harmony, unity, balance, completeness, destructive power, strength, protection, multiple duties, and invincibility.
- The god with six faces: Lord Kartikeya, who has many epithets, such as Muruga, Skanda, Kumara, and Subramanya, is often depicted, in some images, with six faces, each representing a particular divine quality, form of energy, function, or speech,

and collectively, his omnipresence and omniscience. Hence, he is known as Ṣaṭvaktra or Shanmukha.
- The hexagon, Satkona: In the Hindu mandalas and mystic diagrams (yantras), the goddess Durga is often represented by the six-sided hexagon (ṣaṭkona). It is depicted as two interlocking triangles, one pointing upward and the other downward, forming a hexagram. The symbol, used in ritual and tantric worship, also represents the whole creation, an enlightened Shiva yogi, Isvara (who embodies Prakriti), and the union of Shiva and Shakti in tight embrace. According to some, it also symbolizes spiritual awakening, Kundalini energy, and Kartikeya, since he has six faces.
- Shashti: Katyayani, an aspect of Durga, is known as Shashti because she is worshipped on the sixth day (Shashti) during the Navaratri festival, which is celebrated for nine days. Shasti is also revered by mothers in some parts of India and Nepal as the goddess of fertility, childbirth, and the protector of children. According to some accounts, she is said to have participated in Lord Murugan's victory over the demon Soorapadman.
- Shastipurthi: Many Hindus celebrate Shastipurti, the sixtieth birthday of married men in their families, in which their wives, children, friends, and relatives participate. It is celebrated almost like a wedding function if the marriage partner is also alive and both are still living together. The celebration marks a person's marital success, success in life, longevity, victory against the destructive and destabilizing forces of life, and the time for gratitude, reflection, and adjustment.

Seven Saptan

The number seven occupies our thoughts mostly as we remember the days of the week and plan accordingly. It has great symbolic and cultural significance in many cultures and religious traditions since ancient times. It is also found in the symmetry and workings of Nature and popular culture. The rainbow has seven colors, a week has seven days, and the earth has seven continents, seven seas, and seven summits, or the highest mountains. The mind receives knowledge and sensory information through seven channels: two nostrils, two eyes, two ears, and one mouth. The seven stars, also known as the Pleiades, and the seven phases of the moon are powerful universal and occult symbols that have been popular since ancient times.

Whether it is the East or the West, there are seven musical notes. Since ancient times, people across various cultures have observed that seven celestial bodies are visible to the naked eye: the sun, the moon, and five planets, leading them to believe that the number seven holds some mystery and great significance. The Babylonians associated the number with celestial bodies and developed the concept of a seven-day week, a practice later adopted by the Romans, Greeks, and others. The ancient Greeks viewed seven as a complete number, symbolizing perfection, completeness, and harmony. Therefore, they conceived the idea of the Seven Wonders of the World, a tradition that we continue with modern adaptations.

In his book on the occult power and virtues of numbers, W. Wynn Westcott [1] provided a comprehensive account of the significance of various numbers. Regarding the significance of the number seven, he says. "The body has seven obvious parts: the head, chest, abdomen, two legs, and two arms. There are seven internal organs: the stomach, liver, heart, lungs, spleen, and two kidneys. The ruling part, the head, has seven external parts: two eyes, two ears, two nostrils, and a mouth. There are seven things seen: body, interval, magnitude, color, motion, and permanency. There are seven inflections of the voice: the acute, grave, circumflex, rough, smooth, the long, and the short sounds. The hand makes seven motions: up and down, to the right and left, before and behind, and circular. There are seven evacuations: tears from the eyes, mucus from the nostrils, saliva, semen, two excretions, and perspiration. Modern medical knowledge corroborates the ancient dictum that in the seventh month, the human offspring becomes viable. Menstruation tends to occur in a series of four times seven days and is certainly related to Luna in an occult manner. The lyre has seven strings corresponding to the planets. There are seven vowels in English and some other tongues. Theon of Smyrna also notices that the average length of an adult's intestine is 28 feet, four times seven, and 28 is also a perfect number."

He also states that the Assyrian Tablets mention several groups of sevens: the seven gods of the sky, the seven gods of the earth, the seven gods of fiery spheres, the seven maleficent gods, the seven phantoms, the spirits of the seven heavens, and the spirits of the seven earths. In China, the number seven is considered a symbol of death. However, for the Chaldean, seven was a holy number that became harmful or detrimental under certain conditions. The Germanic people, *"Goths had seven Deities from whom come our names of weekdays; Sun, Moon, Tuisco, Wotan, Thor, Friga, Seatur, corresponding, of course, to the planets."*

In Abrahamic religions, the number holds significant symbolic meaning, representing introspection, celebration, wisdom, knowledge, spirituality, completion, perfection, and a connection to God and the cosmos. In Christianity, there are seven sacraments, seven virtues, seven deadly sins, seven laws of Noah, seven archangels, seven trumpets, seven summits, and seven heavens. Based on the Genesis story, the number seven also symbolizes time since God completed creation and brought order out of chaos in seven days. Light, Life, Holiness, Justice, Mercy, Truth, and Love are believed to be the seven spirits or attributes of the Spirit of God, also known as the Holy Ghost [2]. According to the Bible, He completed creation in six days and rested on the seventh day. The first statement on creation in Genesis [3] contains seven words and 28 letters (7 x 4), which reflects the completeness and sacredness of the number seven [4]. The Book of Revelation contains specific references to the seven seals, seven trumpets, and seven bowls, each foreboding the various apocalyptic events that would unfold before Judgement Day.

In Hebrew, seven (shevah) is derived from the root "savah," meaning "to be full or satisfied, to have enough of. ⁵" Accordingly, it is used in Judaism to denote completeness, fullness, or perfection. The menorah, a sacred candelabrum of Jews, has seven branches. It represents divine light and God's presence, and its seven branches symbolize knowledge, creation, and the seven days of the week. The Shabbat day, which falls on the seventh day (from the evening of Friday until nightfall on Saturday), is considered a day of rest and spiritual reflection in Judaism. It symbolizes one's connection to God and the obligation to follow His commandments. The number seven is also important in Islam. The Quran and Hadith mention that Allah created "seven heavens" (sab' samāwāt) and "seven earths" (sab' arāḍīn). Sahih Bukhari describes how they are layered. They signify God's vast creation and the interconnectedness of the cosmos. In many traditions, the number seven is regarded as a symbol of luck, representing affluence and good fortune.

Due to its prevalence in Nature and association with celestial bodies, the number seven has found its way into astrology and numerology. For example, in some schools of Numerology, seven principal numbers are used to determine the influences that may play an important role in a person's life: the soul path number, the personality number, the three predominant name numbers, the destiny number, and the public appearance number. Similarly, the seven traditional planets mentioned above played a crucial role in shaping the classical worldview in astrology since they were conceived as celestial guides influencing human lives, natural phenomena, and the cosmos itself. Each of them was associated with a deity and specific qualities and influences.

The number seven also has mathematical significance due to its unique nature. It is the fourth prime number, after 2, 3, and 5, which can only be divided by one or itself. It is an odd number that lies between two perfect squares, 4 (2^2) and 9 (3^2), which makes it a "central" prime in a way. Geometrically, the number seven represents a heptagon. However, it is a unique geometrical symmetry or form, as one cannot construct a seven-sided polygon or a heptagon with a compass and a straightedge, which makes it mysterious and mystical. Seven is the most frequent sum that comes up when rolling two six-sided dice since there are six ways to achieve it (1+6, 2+5, 3+4, and their reverses). Hence, it is considered a lucky number. In the Fibonacci sequence of numbers, seven is closely linked to the patterns that appear in Nature and growth or multiplication. In number theory, seven is one of the lucky numbers generated through a sieving process similar to the one used in mathematics to find prime numbers. They are used in cryptographic algorithms for generating random or pseudorandom numbers.

Significance in Hinduism

In Hinduism, the number seven holds profound significance in ritual and spiritual practices, representing both unity and diversity within the cosmic order, as well as the connection between God and His creation. For devotees, each day of the week carries religious significance as auspicious or inauspicious or suitable or unsuitable for worshipping certain deities. For example, many Hindus worship Shiva on Mondays, gurus and some seers on Thursdays, the Goddesses on Fridays, and Balaji on Saturdays. Some people practice fasting, visit temples to offer worship, and avoid eating meat on these days. At the highest level, the number represents the mortal world, the seventh in the cosmic hierarchy of the 14 spheres of the cosmos. In all, there are said to be 14 spheres or worlds, of which six are above the Earth and seven are below it. Above them is the transcendental world, the immortal world of Brahman, the Zero. If we include it, the worlds become 15, with the Earth placed exactly in the middle, with seven above (including the zero plane) and seven below.

The Cosmic Order of Hinduism underwent many changes in its long history. For example, Chandogya Upanishad and the Gayatri mantra mention three worlds: the mortal world (bhur or bhuloka), the middle world or mid-region (bhuvarloka), and heaven (suva, svara, or svargaloka). The first world is inhabited by mortal beings, the second by celestial beings, and the third by the devas or gods ruled by Indra. This is the most traditional view of Hindu cosmology found in the literature of the early Vedic period. However, in the Puranas and the extended version of the Gayatri mantra, we find descriptions of additional worlds above Indra's heaven: Maharloka (the world of radiant beings), Janaloka (the world of deities), Tapoloka (the world of pure souls), and Satyaloka or Brahmaloka (the world of Truth). These seven worlds are also said to correspond to the seven planes of consciousness or the sheaths in our bodies: the physical plane (annamaya) with earth, the breath plane (pranamaya) with bhuva, the mental plane (manomaya) with svarga, the plane of intelligence (vijnanamaya) with Mahar, the plane of latent divinities with janah, the radiant plane of spiritual fire with tapa, and the supreme consciousness of Atman itself with Brahma.

While there are six planes above the earth, there are seven below: Atala, Vitala, Sutala, Mahatala, Tatatala, Rasatala, and Patala. These underworlds are filled with darkness and inhabited by Asuras, Danavas, Daityas, Rakshasas, and other evil forces. The human body, often regarded as a symbolic microcosm, contains miniature versions of these fourteen planes. The following table shows the correlation between the seven chakras, the seven body sheaths, and the seven higher and lower worlds.

Higher Organ	Higher World	Chakra	Body Sheath	Lower Organ	Lower World
Navel	Earth	Muladhara	Anna	Hips	Atala
Abdomen	Bhuvah	Svadhishtana	Prana	Thighs	Vitala
Heart	Suvah	Manipura	Mano	Knees	Sutala
Throat	Mahar	Anahata	Vignana	Calves	Talatala
Mouth	Jana	Visuddha	Janah	Ankles	Rasatala
Brain	Tapah	Ajna	Tapo	Feet	Mahatala
Top of the skull	Satya	Sahasrara	Brahma	Soles of the feet	Patala

Hindu Puranas, such as the Vishnu Purana, describe the cosmology and geography of planet Earth as having seven concentric islands (or continents): Jambu, Shaka, Kusha, Krauncha, Shalmali, Pluksha, and Pushkara. According to the descriptions found in them, each island has distinct characteristics and is ruled by a specific deity. Seven concentric oceans (Saptadvipa), each made of a different material, separate them from each other: Lavana (salt), Ikshu (sugarcane juice), Sura (wine), Ghrita (clarified butter), Dadhi (yogurt), Rasa (sap or juice), and Jala (water). They represent the diverse manifestations of God's infinite abundance. We now know that this cannot be true in a physical sense. This representation of our world is either symbolic or belongs to a subtle plane.

Brahman, the highest, supreme Deity of Hinduism, who represents the highest, eternal, and indestructible reality, has the epithet of "Saptātman" since He is said to manifest in seven different forms, states or aspects, each symbolizing a different dimension of existence and creation, and representing the interconnectedness, order, and diversity of creation. While we do not have a specific answer why He is called so, we may presume that it may be because, in creation, He manifests differently as the Word (Akshara), Food or materiality (Annam), Sound (svara or nada), Energy (Prana), Light (prakash), Intelligence (prajna), and Chaitanya (consciousness). Each of these may manifest further in different forms. For example, "Word" may also refer to speech, the alphabet, languages, and so on. "Food" means every object in creation that is subject to impermanence and serves as nourishment for the mind and senses or the body. "Sound" may include all the sounds that manifest in creation, including the sounds arising from the utterance of sacred syllables such as Aum, Hrim, and mantras. "Energy" represents Prana and encompasses both the gross and subtle energies of Shakti, or the Goddess, which are found in the body and creation.

Hindu scriptures mention the number seven (sapta) in connection with many other aspects of Brahman and His Creation. For example, Surya, the sun god, rides on a chariot yoked by seven horses, each corresponding to a particular color, energy, and day in the week. The Mundaka Upanishad refers to seven tongues (sapta jivhas), flames, or forms of Agni, namely Kali (black), Karali (fierce), Manojava (swift as mind), Sulohita (red as iron), Sudhumravarna (smoke-colored), Visharuch-Devi (universally pleasing), and Sphulingini (cracking). In the iconography of Agni, they are depicted as his seven hands. In the human body, they may represent the seven bodily tissues (sapta dhatus), namely plasma, blood, muscle, fat, bone, marrow, and reproductive tissue, and the seven digestive fires associated with each of the seven Dhatus, namely Jatharajni (the central digestive fire), Bhutagni (the five elemental fires), and Dhatvagni. They may also correspond to the higher energies, the seven states of consciousness, and the seven states of self-absorption that one experiences in the advanced state of spiritual practice when the mind and body are purified and disciplined.

The Durga Saptashati, also known as the Devi Mahatmya or Chandi Path, which is a part of the Markandeya Purana, describes seven forms of the goddess Durga, popularly known as Saptamatrikas or the Seven Mothers, which manifested when she fought ferociously with a demon named Raktabija. They are Brahmani, Maheshwari or Shivani, Kaumari, Vaishnavi, Varahi, Chamundi or Narasimhi, and Aindri. As their names suggest, they are the powers or energies of Isvara, the Lord of the Universe, each associated with a particular functional aspect of Him, namely Brahma, Shiva, Skanda, Vishnu, Varaha, Narasimha, and Indra, respectively. According to the Hindu Tantras, these seven Shaktis correspond to the seven subtle energies of the mind and body, as shown below.

Name of Shakti	Corresponding energy in the body
Brahmi	The awakening power. She is latent in the Pranava Nada or the primal sound AUM.
Vaishnavi	The organizing power. She creates beauty and symmetry in the beings.
Maheshwari	The concealing power. She creates a sense of individuality in the beings.
Kaumari	The awakening power. She creates an intense aspiration for spiritual liberation in the beings and leads them to a guru for enlightenment.
Varahi	The assimilating power. She allows beings to enjoy foods and energies of various kinds.
Aindri	The conscientious power. She removes or weakens

	the sensory opposition to the perceived moral code.
Chamundi	The controlling power. She controls the modifications of the mind and facilitates withdrawal, equanimity, and concentration.

Apart from the above, the number seven is associated with the following important concepts also in Hinduism.

- The Saptarishis or Seven Seers: According to Hindu scriptures, Brahma transmitted the knowledge of the Vedas initially through seven seers known as the Saptarishis. They played a significant role in preserving and propagating the Vedas and the ritual practices associated with them for the benefit of humanity. Their names are not definitive. One version contains the following seven names: Atri, Bharadvaja, Gautama, Jamadagni, Kashyapa, Vashishta, and Vishwamitra. In some versions, Agastya and Pulastya are also included. They are symbolically associated with the seven stars in the constellation of Ursa Major, signifying their eternal presence in God's creation, and are said to remain active for the duration of the current Manvantara, which lasts approximately 306.5 million Earth years, disseminating spiritual knowledge and guiding humanity.
- The seven musical notes: Isvara, the Lord of the Universe, is the source and controller of all the svaras: musical notes, sounds, vibrations, speech, languages, words, and letters of the alphabet. The Sapta Svaras, or the seven musical notes - Sa, Re, Ga, Ma, Pa, Da, and Ni - constitute the Octave (Saptak) and are foundational to classical Indian music, encompassing both Carnatic and Hindustani music. They also symbolically represent the universal order, balance, and regularity (Rta), the hidden sound (Aantarghosha), and the subtle sound (Nada), which flow continuously in the subtle space and are audible only to those who transcend their minds and senses and enter the deep and indistinguishable silence. Indian classical music is an integral part of Hindu spirituality and is closely tied to devotional practices, serving as a medium of devotion and worship.

- Seven islands and seven oceans: As already discussed before, Puranas, such as the Vishnu Purana, Bhagavata Purana, and Matsya Purana, describe seven concentric islands, each governed by a specific deity and separated by seven oceans composed of distinct substances, including water, salt water, milk, and others. The seven islands symbolize the seven stages (pranta bhumi) of insight (prajna) in Yoga, known as Saptada, or the seven stages of insightful awareness one enters during mindful meditation [6].
- Sapta Srishti or the Sevenfold Creation of Brahman: The Puranas and Upanishads describe the sevenfold creation of Brahman, namely the Primary Creation (Mahad Srishti), Subtle Elemental Creation (Tanmatra Srishti), Gross Elemental Creation (Bhuta Srishti), Creation of Senses (Indriya Srishti), Creation of Beings (Jiva Srishti), Creation of Humans (Manushya Srishti), and Creation of Gods (Deva Srishti). These seven creations proceed from the subtle to the gross and from the formless to the formed. They denote the divine origin of all things and their interconnectedness, suggesting how, in our spiritual progress or liberation, we must proceed from the gross to the subtle and from the formed to the formless to attain liberation from samsara.
- Saptapadi: Hindu marriages involve a sacred ritual called Saptapadi, in which the bride and groom walk seven steps together, locking their small fingers and taking seven vows while circling the sacred fire in the presence of all the guests, officiating priests, and the gods invoked to witness the marriage and accept the offerings. Furthermore, it is said that Hindu marriages are not just between two individuals but between two souls who have been brought together by the gods to uphold Dharma and nourish them through sacrifices. Their relationship is believed to last for seven consecutive lives.
- Saptachakras: The human body is a powerhouse of energy, ruled by Shakti and her numerous manifestations. Energy flows continuously through various subtle channels in the body as prana, the vital energy. Hindu scriptures of the Tantra allude to seven subtle chakras located between the base of the

spine and the head region, through which the Kundalini energy passes when it is energized and awakened. The seven chakras are Muladhara (Root Chakra), Svadhisthana (Sacral Chakra), Manipura (Solar Plexus Chakra), Anahata (Heart Chakra), Vishuddha (Throat Chakra), Ajna (Third Eye Chakra), and Sahasrara (Crown Chakra). They are believed to play a crucial role in the physical, mental, and spiritual well-being of practicing yogis, facilitating their spiritual development, self-purification, and self-realization.
- Sapta Prakriti: Arthashastra and Manusmriti refer to seven constituent parts of a king's administrative or governing body, namely Swami (The King), Amatya (The Ministers), Janapada (The Territory and People), Durga (The Fortified City), Kosha (The Treasury), Danda (The Army), and Mitra (The Allies). They are vital to the proper functioning of
- Sapta Jnana Bhumikas, or the Seven Stages of Knowledge: According to Yoga Vasistha and Varaha Upanishad, seekers of liberation progress through seven distinct stages of spiritual development, gaining increased knowledge and awareness at each stage until they culminate in self-realization. These seven stages serve as a blueprint for spiritual seekers, guiding them from ignorance to enlightenment and helping them attain self-purification and inner transformation through dedicated effort, resolve, and self-discipline. The seven stages are: Shubheccha: Development of a strong desire; Vicharana: Engaging in study, reflection, and deep inquiry; Tanmanasa: Purifying and developing a subtle mind that is free from distractions, desires, and attachments; Sattvapatti: Attainment of purity, equanimity, and detachment by overcoming ego and other impurities; Asamshakti: Developing sameness and complete detachment and freedom from the world, its dualities, and delusion; Padarthabhavana: Seeing things as they are without duality, division, or objectivity; and Turyaga: Attaining complete liberation or transcendence by merging with the ultimate reality of Brahman.
- Saptami: The seventh day of the fortnight in the Hindu lunar calendar is known as Saptami. It holds religious and spiritual

significance to Hindus, as it is connected to Surya, the sun god. The famous Hindu festival, Ratha Saptami, is celebrated on this day, signifying the northward journey (Uttrayana) of the sun, marking the change of seasons and the journey of liberated souls to the immortal world. Bhanu Saptami, Durga Saptami (observed during the Navaratri festival), and Vijaya Saptami (commemorating Lord Rama's victory in battle) are also celebrated on this day in various parts of India.

In addition to the above, the following concepts associated with the number seven are also important.

- Sapta Nadi Chakra: A diagram used in Hindu astrology to predict weather (rain) and planetary influences. The concept may also refer to the seven Chakras or the seven nerve channels through which vital energy flows in the body.
- Sapta Puris: The seven holiest cities that are worthy of pilgrimage to cleanse sins, namely, Kashi, Varanasi, Mathura or Haridwar, Ayodhya, Dwarka, Ujjain, and Avantika.
- Sapta Badris: The seven sacred places dedicated to Lord Vishnu in the Garhwal region of the Himalayas, known as Badri Kshetra, namely Sri Badrinath Dham, Adi Badri, Bhavishya Badri, Vrddha Badri, Yoga Badri, Dhyan Badri, and Nrsinga Badri.
- Saptanadis: The seven most sacred rivers of India, worshipped by Hindus, namely Ganga, Yamuna, Godavari, Saraswathi, Narmada, Sindhu, and Kaveri, are grouped under this name.
- Sapta Kshetras: The seven battlefields that witnessed conflicts between good and evil. The names vary. One version contains the following: Kurukshetra, Purushottama Kshetra, Harihara Kshetra, Prabha Kshetra, Ram Kshetra, Bhunga Kshetra, and Sukar Kshetra. Some lists include Lanka, Khandava Vana, Pragjyotisha, Mathura, Tripura, and Dwaraka.
- Saptabhangi: The concept of seven perspectives or viewpoints in Jain philosophy, according to which truths are complex and must be examined from different perspectives or viewpoints to gain the right understanding.

- Sapta Bhangima: The seven types of body postures or stances that are used in Indian classical dance, particularly Bharatanatyam, to convey emotions, aesthetics, and storylines. The postures are integral to the art forms and are designed to create visual harmony between emotions and expressions. The seven postures often involve proper alignment of the mind and body, involving the head, neck, torso, and limbs, each contributing to the overall narrative and beauty of the performance.

Reference

1. Westcott Wynn, W, Collectanea Hermetica Vol. IX. Numbers, Their Occult Power And Mystic Virtues, Third Edition, 1911, London, Theosophical Publishing Society.
2. Alford L. A Rev, Mystic Numbers of the Word or Five Hundred Important Theological and Scientific Questions Answered, 1870, Longsport Ind.: L.A. Alford & Sons.
3. In the beginning, God created the heavens and the earth.
4. Coffman, C. J. Manual of the Enumeration: A Textbook on the Sciences of the Enumeration. Los Angeles, California: Dean of the Enumeration, 1927. Project Gutenberg eBook, 2011.
5. Ethelbert\Bullinger V., D.D. Number In Scripture, Its Supernatural Design And Spiritual Significance, Second Edition, 1895, Messrs. Eyre And Spottiswood, Great New Street, London, E.C.
6. Patanjali, Yogasutras, 2.27.

Eight, Ashtan

Number eight signifies many things in various cultures: infinity, continuity, prosperity, balance, harmony, and the union of opposites. Technically, eight is the first day that comes at the end of every week. Thus, it symbolizes continuity, regeneration, resurrection, and rebirth. According to Wikipedia, since the cardinal number 7 is the highest number of items that can universally and cognitively be processed as a single set, one might argue that the etymology of the numeral eight could be viewed as the first number to be considered composite, either as "twice four" or as "two short of ten," or something similar. This argument is supported by the fact that in some cultures, the number eight was used in the sense of twice four or two short of ten. The modern digit 8 developed from the original Brahmi digit. Although it is considered a symbol of infinity, the actual infinity symbol (∞) resembles a "sideways eight" and is said to have originated independently.

Geometrically, eight is represented by an octagon or an eight-sided polygon. In computer programming, eight binary digits (bits) constitute one byte, the basic data unit referenced in old processors, memory representation, character encoding, and graphics. In Nature, eight corresponds to the atomic number [1] of Oxygen. Most spiders, scorpions, mites, and ticks are eight-legged, and Octopuses, squids, and lobsters possess eight legs or tentacles. The human body has eight cervical nerves, eight carpal bones, eight lobes or functional segments in the liver, eight major endocrine glands, eight bones in the cranium, and eight major nerve pathways. The human embryo undergoes critical development and develops major organs in the first eight weeks. Furthermore, Science acknowledges eight essential B vitamins that are crucial for metabolism and overall health, eight phases of the moon in each lunar cycle, and eight major planets in the solar system [2]. According to the octet rule in chemistry, atoms achieve stability by having at least eight electrons in their outer shell.

The number eight had significance in many ancient cultures. For the Babylonians and Assyrians, it represented celestial harmony, balance, and cosmic order. They divided the heavens into eight zones, just as the ancient Vedic people divided space into eight directions and eight zones, each ruled by a deity. The Greeks venerated it as a symbol of balance and regeneration. They thought that it was "an all-powerful number." Hence, they had the Proverb, "all things are eight." [3]

The Pythagoreans regarded it as a symbol of the goddess Venus, associating it with love, harmony, and friendship. They held that humans possessed eight faculties: sense, fantasy, art, opinion, prudence, science, wisdom, and mind [4]. The concept of the Ogdoad, found in Greek Mythology and Egyptian cosmology, refers to a group of eight primordial deities that embody the fundamental elements of creation and the balance of the universe. The eight primordial deities, comprising four male and four female deities, represent the union or coexistence of dualities or pairs of opposites, such as light and darkness, male and female, and happiness and sorrow. They signify that the universe is a playground of diverse complementary forces working together in balance, where order and harmony prevail amidst chaos and uncertainty.

The Romans shared similar ideas, viewing eight as a symbol of the cyclical nature of life and rebirth. They incorporated octagonal structures profusely into their architecture, such as baptisteries, mausoleums, tombs, domes, and rotundas, and viewed them not only as aesthetically appealing structures but also as symbols of the connection between the mortals and the immortals, spiritual renewal, and the promise of eternal life. The octagonal design found its way into other architectural traditions, including Byzantine and Islamic architecture. Similar views prevail in many other cultures, where the number eight represents infinity, eternal cycles, balance, and the coexistence of opposites.

In Hebrew, eight (Sh'moneh) means superabundance of oil, fat, fertility, or something. It is the day that came after the completion of God's perfect creation. Hence, it represents a new beginning or a new chapter in human existence, the start of a new era, or a new order of things. Jews celebrate Hanukkah, also known as the Festival of Lights, over eight days in memory of the rededication of the Holy

Temple in Jerusalem and the miracle of the oil that burned for eight days, despite there being enough for only one day. They also traditionally practice circumcision on male infants on the 8th day after birth.

In Christianity, the number represents resurrection and salvation, as Jesus rose on the eighth day, the day after the Sabbath. Additionally, the eight Beatitudes, spoken by Jesus during the Sermon on the Mount, as recorded in the Gospel of Matthew (Matthew 5:3-12), serve as the cornerstone of Christian teachings. They embody Christian values and provide guidance to the faithful for living a life of faith, love, and service.

In Buddhism, the Buddha preached the Eightfold Path, comprising eight principles for righteous living that lead to purification, equanimity, and insightful awareness, and Nirvana or permanent liberation from suffering. They are symbolized as the eight spokes of the Dharma Wheel. In Chinese numerology, the number eight symbolizes prosperity and good fortune. In medieval times, European astrologers attributed the number eight to the unmoving stars in the cosmos, a view that was influenced by Aristotelian and Ptolemaic astronomy. They believed that the fixed stars influenced planetary energy, serving as a fitting symbol of celestial harmony and channeled divine or cosmic perfection.

In Hinduism, the number eight holds deep symbolic significance and is associated with many important concepts, divinities, beliefs, and practices. The following examples amply illustrate its significance.

- Ashtadikpalas: The Ashtadikpalas are lords of heaven who rule the eight directions (dik) or divisions of space, each serving as a divine Lord (dikpala). They are Indra (the eastern Lord), Varuna (the western Lord), Kubera (the northern Lord), Yama (the southern Lord), Agni (the southeastern Lord), Niruthi (the southwestern Lord), Isana (the northeastern Lord), and Vayu (the northwestern Lord. They are the original and highest gods of the Vedic pantheon but were subsequently relegated to a secondary level as the guardians of space due to changes within Vedic religion and the emergence of more popular and powerful deities in Vaishnavism, Shaivism, and Shaktism. They symbolize the divine nature manifesting in diverse forms and potencies, representing the interconnectedness of creation and the all-pervading, divine presence and power. They are still invoked in Hindu temples and rituals. They also play a prominent role in Hindu Vaastu Shastra, the building manuals that stipulate guidelines for the selection of the land, location, layout, design, and construction of Hindu temples and secular buildings.

- Adityas: The earliest hymns of the Rigveda mention eight solar gods, known as Adityas, who were born to the sage Kashyapa and Aditi, the "mother of gods," who personifies the infinite and boundless. They are Varuna, Mitra, Aryaman, Bhaga, Ansha, Daksha, Indra, and Martanda. An alternative list is also in circulation, consisting of Mitra, Varuna, Aryaman, Amia, Bhaga, Dhatar, Indra, and Vaivasvan. The later Vedic texts expanded the number to 12, likely to correspond with the 12 months of the Hindu lunar calendar: Mitra, Varuna, Aryaman, Bhaga, Daksha, Anshuman, Surya, Vivasvan, Tvashtar, and Vishnu.

- Rudras: The Vedas extol the storm gods of thunder and rain, known as Rudras, meaning the roaring, raging, and howling ones. They are also often described as the manifestations or associate deities of Shiva or Rudra. The Vedic people feared them as harbingers of calamities, sickness, death, and the destruction of cattle, crops, lives, harvests, and houses, causing unmitigable suffering when displeased. Hence, they often invoked them in Vedic rituals for protection and blessings. Their number also varies from eight to eleven. The Taittiriya Samhita of the Yajurveda mentions their number as eight. However, in subsequent accounts, their number rose to 11.

- Ashtamurthi: Lord Shiva is known as Ashtamurthi because he has eight forms, each with distinct names, qualities, and functions: Bhava, Sarva, Isana, Pasupati, Bhima, Ugra, Mahadeva, and Rudra. They denote Shiva's omniscient, omnipotent, universal, and absolute aspects as Brahman or Isvara, the Supreme Lord of the Universe, who pervades and controls every aspect of creation. For example, Bhava represents existence and creation; Sarva signifies Shiva's all-pervading nature or omnipresence; Isana denotes mastery, sovereignty, and spiritual guidance; Pasupati represents lordship over all living beings; Bhima represents Shiva's infinite and indomitable power; Ugra symbolizes Shiva's fierce aspects and his role in purification and spiritual transformation; Mahadeva denotes Shiva's sovereign and supreme power as the Lord of all; and Rudra symbolizes the cosmic force of destruction and renewal.

- Ashtalakshmi: Goddess Lakshmi, the goddess of wealth and abundance and the consort of Lord Vishnu, is revered in Hindu scriptures and devotional prayers as having eight forms or manifestations, each serving a distinct function in the cosmos in her role as the Universal Mother, Primal Goddess, and Mother of all. They are Adi Lakshmi (primal goddess), Dhanya Lakshmi (goddess of food and agricultural wealth), Dhairya Lakshmi (goddess of courage, valor, and fearlessness), Gaja Lakshmi (goddess of the power, majesty, and opulence of elephants), Santana Lakshmi (bestower of fertility and the wealth of children), Vijaya Lakshmi (bestower of the wealth of success and victory in all undertaking). Vidya Lakshmi (goddess of the wealth of knowledge) and Dhana Lakshmi (goddess of material wealth). Worshipping and invoking these eight forms of the goddess, devotees seek a harmonious and fulfilling life as well as material, spiritual, emotional, and intellectual wealth and well-being.

- Ashta Shaktis: They are the eight supreme powers or potencies (Shaktis) of Lord Vishnu in his aspect as Narayana, Maha Vishnu, or Isvara (the Lord of the Universe). They are Sridevi (goddess of wealth and good fortune), Bhudevi (goddess of the earth), Saraswathi (goddess of knowledge), Priti (goddess of kindness and happiness), Kirti (goddess of fame and distinction), Shanti (goddess of peace and harmony), Tusti (goddess of pleasure and satisfaction) and Pusti (goddess of strength, vigor, and health).

- Ashta Mahishis: According to the Bhagavata Purana, Harivamsa, Vishnu Purana, and Mahabharata, Lord Krishna had eight principal consorts, known as Patta Mahishis or consecrated wives, or queens. They are Rukmini, Satyabhama, Jambavati, Kalindi, Mitravinda, Nagnajiti or Satya, Bhadra, and

Lakshmana or Madri. Like the above-mentioned Ashta Shaktis, they embody different qualities that complement Lord Krishna's supreme splendor and divine nature in his role as a divine incarnation, lover, protector, teacher, controller, and bestower of grace and liberation upon his exclusive devotees.
- Ashta Vasus: According to the Vedas, Puranas, and the Mahabharata, Indra has eight attendants known as the Ashta Vasus, each symbolizing a particular aspect of Indra's radiance, lordship, opulence, and power. In spirituality, they represent the natural forces of creation that uphold both the physical and spiritual worlds, maintaining balance and harmony. Symbolically, they represent the eight components of the internal organ (antahkarana), namely the five senses, the mind, the ego, and the organ of intelligence. The eight Vasus are Dhara (the earth), Anala (the fire), Apa (the waters), Anila (the wind), Dhruva (the north star), Soma (the moon), Prabhasa (the daylight), and Pratyusha (the dawn).
- Eight pleasant and fierce forms of Lord Shiva: We have already discussed the eight forms of Lord Shiva. Apart from them, the Shaiva Puranas and other texts describe eight of his pleasant (saumya) and fierce (ugra) forms. The eight peaceful forms are Saumya or Anugraha Murthi, Ugra or Rudra or Samhara Murthi, Nritta or Tandava Murthi, Dakshinamurthy, Lingodbhava Murthi, Bhikshatana Murthi, Haryardha Murthi, and Ardhanariswara Murthi. His eight terrible forms are Kankala Bhairava, Gajasuravadha Murthi, Tripurantaka Murthi, Sarabhesvara Murthi, Kalari Murthi, Kamantaka Murthi, and Andhakasura Vadha Murthi. These diverse manifestations reflect Shiva's supreme powers and potencies as the Universal Lord and source of all, who performs five universal functions: creation, preservation, destruction, concealment, and revelation.
- Ashtadala-Padma Lingam: The Shivalingam, Lord Shiva's iconic representation, symbolizes the eight-petalled lotus (padma). Hence, the expression in one of the famous invocations addressed to him – "*ashtadala pariveshtitha lingam.*" It also represents the union of the spiritual and material or the

transcendental and temporal, as represented by Shiva and Shakti, respectively. The lotus signifies purity (shivam), beauty and harmony (sundaram), and the supreme reality (satyam) of Lord Shiva. It also stands for the entire creation arising from Shiva, with him acting as the center (Bindu) or the lingam. The eight petals represent his eight supreme manifestations, eight pleasant and fierce forms, and the eightfold progress of yogis on the path of liberation, culminating in enlightenment and oneness with Shiva's pure and auspicious state, the center. They also epitomize the sacred geometry seen in the design of Hindu temples and the yantras (mystical diagrams) used in Tantric rituals.

- Shashtanga Namaskaram: It is a traditional form of prostration or salutation in Hindu rituals and devotional practices performed by kneeling, prostrating, and worshipping or expressing gratitude with eight (sashta) parts (anga) of the body: two hands, two feet, two knees, the chest, and the forehead. It denotes complete and unconditional devotion, humility, and surrender to a deity, teacher, or an elderly person while letting go of pride and ego. Similar practices are also found in other cultures and religions, including Buddhism, Shintoism, Islam, and Christianity, as well as Native American and Tibetan spiritual traditions.
- Shastanga Yoga: The Classical Indian Yoga of Patanjali is also known as Shashtanga Yoga since it contains eight methods or practices known as parts or Angas, namely Yama (control), Niyama (rules), Asana (postures), Pranayama (breathing practice), Pratyahara (withdrawal of senses), Dharana (concentration), Dhyana (meditation) and Samadhi (self-absorption).
- Ashta Aiswaryas and Ashta Daridryas: Both these refer to the eight forms of good fortune and the eight forms of adversity people face in their lives. The eight forms of good fortune (ashtaiswaryas) are bestowed upon her devotees by the eight manifestations of the goddess Lakshmi. The latter refers to the eight types of misfortunes or adversity (ashta daridyas): poverty of knowledge or wisdom, poverty of wealth or material resources, poverty of health or physical well-being, poverty of prosperity

or success, poverty of courage or valor, poverty of peace or tranquility, poverty of devotion or faith, and poverty of liberation or spiritual freedom. They may arise due to fate, karma, or the lack of divine grace and are collectively represented by the goddess known as Alakshmi or Jyestha Devi, who has several other names and is believed to be the elder sister of Goddess Lakshmi.

Apart from the above, we also find collections of eight in various Hindu texts, which denote unity, diversity, strength, and wholesome qualities associated with the number eight, such as the following.

- Eight types of sexual enjoyment.
- Eight duties of a king.
- Eight qualities of a Brahman.
- Eight ears of Brahma.
- Eight elephants that stand around the earth, guarding the eight quarters.
- Ashtadhatu, an alloy made of eight metals: gold, silver, copper, iron, tin, lead, zinc, and mercury.
- Eight auspicious encounters or visions.
- Eight rasas or emotions of a drama: love, humor, sadness, anger, courage, fear, horror, and wonder.
- Eight methods of ritual worship, using water, sandal paste, flowers, incense, light, grains, sweets, and fruit.
- Eight forms of Ganesha: Mahaganapati, Varada-Vinayaka, Chintamani Vinayaka, Girijatmaja Vinayaka, Vghneswara, Bala Vinayaka and Siddhi Vinayaka.

References

1. The number of protons in the nucleus of an atom of that element.
2. The status of the ninth planet, Pluto, is disputed.
3. Westcott Wynn, W, Collectanea Hermetica Vol. IX. Numbers, Their Occult Power And Mystic Virtues, Third Edition, 1911, London, Theosophical Publishing Society.
4. Barrett, Francis. The Magus, or Celestial Intelligencer: Being a Complete System of Occult Philosophy. London: Lackington, Allen & Co., 1801. Available at Archive.org.

Nine, Navan

Nine is the last and highest single-digit number in the decimal system, possessing unique properties. For example, it is the first square of an odd number. A number is divisible by nine if the sum of its digits is also divisible by nine. The multiples of nine (e.g., 9×1=9, 9×2=18, 9×3=27, etc.) always sum up to 9 (e.g., 1+8=9, 2+7=9). Similarly, the sum of the digits of any number multiplied by 9 always reduces to 9, as shown in the following table. This shows that nine reproduces itself in several instances. That makes it similar to all-natural recurring phenomena found in Nature, such as the ego, creation, and anything that reproduces itself.

9x4	36	3+6 = 9
9x9	81	8+1 =9
9x72	648	6+4+8=18 - 1+8=9
9x456	4104	4+1+0+4 =9
9x345	3105	3+1+0+5=9
9x789	7101	7+1+0+1=9
9x5387	48483	4+8+4+8+3 = 27 – 2+7=9
9x39281	353529	3+5+3+5+2=18 – 1+8 =9
9x254867	2293803	2+2+9+3+8+0+3=27 – 2+7=9
9x4897654	44078886	4+4+0+7+8+8+8+6 =45 – 4+5=9

Nine is the highest of the single digits but falls short of 10, signifying the outer limits of all finite phenomena, including the physical world and the objective reality we experience through our minds and senses. In this way, it symbolizes creation, manifestation, and the material universe. Indeed, it represents the sum of all manifested and limited aspects and realities, because, however large or infinite they may seem, they are still limited, definitive, and finite, each with a beginning and an end. There is always a finality to what can be, what is possible, or what one may accomplish with created things and creation itself. Hence, the number nine is comparable to objective reality and the horizon because both have limitations despite their vastness. Further, although it is the highest, it is still short of the perfection and completeness we seek to attain in our lives. Still, it is an important milestone in our achievements, since it brings us to the edge of the goals we seek and things we desire, propelling and motivating us to persevere and transcend ourselves.

Nine is also comparable to the human mind and intelligence, since they represent the pinnacle of evolution on Earth, but fall short of the cosmic heights to which humans can evolve through spiritual effort. There is a finality to what we can accomplish within a limited lifespan and our limited faculties and resources. As humans, we possess great potential to achieve many great things and attain stupendous success in our lives. However, ultimately, we must face death and our impermanence, which puts a cap on what we can achieve or what progress or success we can accomplish in our lives. Like those who lived in the past, we will eventually end up in the graveyard of the Earth's lost memories. The number nine faces the same predicament. It has a limitation despite being the highest among the digits, and cannot surpass itself unless it joins with other numbers and loses its identity. Being one short of 10, it is almost complete, yet not entirely so, and nearly perfect, yet not quite. This way, the number nine also represents human beings. Although they are made in the image of God and arise due to the union of Purusha and Prakriti, just as Isvara is, they are still short of perfection. It is also comparable to Atman, the individual Self. It is divine, eternal, indestructible, and independent, but not as exalted as Brahman, the Supreme Self. Hence, the Vishistadvaita (Qualified Nondualism) School of Hinduism proposes the bheda-abheda doctrine, according to which the individual Self is both similar to (abheda) and dissimilar (bheda) from Brahman.

Similar themes about the significance of the number nine also prevail in popular culture, where it symbolizes the upper limit of a concept, possibility, potential, or phenomenon, which is also well expressed in idiomatic expressions such as "the whole nine yards," "the nine lives of a cat," "to be on cloud nine," and "dressed to the nines." Thus, nine symbolizes all near-perfect things in creation, just as humans who are similar to gods but not equal to them, who are well-qualified to achieve immortality but do not find it easy or succeed much in attaining it. Perhaps for this reason, the Greeks attributed the number to Prometheus, who symbolizes human striving for innovation, excellence, knowledge, and perfection. Prometheus wanted to help humanity by stealing fire from Mount Olympus and giving it to humanity against the wishes of Zeus. Angered by his impudence, Zeus punished him by binding him to a rock and setting an eagle upon him that ate his liver every day.

The number nine was prominent in ancient and primitive cultures. They often associated the number with sacred geometry and cosmic patterns, such as the circle, which represented infinity and wholeness, with its 360 degrees that can be reduced to nine. Some ancient cultures practiced burying their dead after nine days. The custom still continues in some communities and is widely documented [1]. The Ancient Greeks believed in nine Muses, daughters of Zeus and goddesses of inspiration, who presided over the arts, literature, and sciences. They were believed to be responsible for the great works of art produced by their writers, poets, philosophers, and artists. The ancient Romans worshipped nine Sabine gods, known as Novensiles or Novensides: Hercules, Romulus, Aesculapius, Bacchus, Aeneas, Vesta, Fortuna, and Fides. The Etruscans, who established an ancient civilization in central Italy during the pre-Roman days (around 900 BCE to 27 BCE), also worshipped nine gods: Juno, Minerva, Tinia, Vulcan, Mars, Saturn, Hercules, Summanus, and Vedius. The Romans performed a purification ceremony on male infants on the ninth day after their birth, making offerings to the goddess Nundina. The number nine is also significant in Freemasonry. The "Nine Elected Knights," also known as the "Master Elect of Nine," is the ninth degree in the Ancient and Accepted Scottish Rite of Freemasonry. The number nine is central to this degree, representing completeness and the pursuit of higher knowledge. Christian theologians, such as Pope Saint Gregory and Saint Paul, described nine orders (or classes) of Angels: Seraphim, Cherubim, Thrones, Dominions, Virtues, Powers, Principalities, Archangels, and Angels. In Islam, Allah has 99 names. Some Jewish teachings suggest that God has descended to the earth nine times and will descend again at the time of the apocalypse, which will be His final descent.

Because of its spiritual and cultural significance, the number nine is integrated into the ritual and ceremonial practices of many Eastern Cultures. In China, the number is associated with the indomitable power of the dragon and the majesty and sovereignty of emperors. It also represents longevity, eternity, and completeness, and is often used in rituals and ceremonies to convey wishes for a long and prosperous life. During birthdays or weddings, gifts are given in multiples of nine or sets of nine to signify the abundance, prosperity, and generosity of the donors, as well as good fortune and blessings for the recipient. Monetary gifts are also given in nines or in sets of nine (such as 9, 99, 999) for the same reason. In Japanese culture, the number nine has mixed connotations, as the word shares a phonetic similarity with the word "ku," which means suffering. Still, in certain traditional contexts, such as tea ceremonies or artistic arrangements, odd numbers like nine are considered aesthetically pleasing, auspicious, and harmonious. The Ifugao, an Indigenous ethnic group from the mountainous region of northern Luzon in the Philippines, perform rituals related to agricultural practices, life stages, and spiritual beliefs that involve specific numbers, including nine, to represent completeness and balance.

In science, it also appears in various disciplines and contexts, denoting its distinction. For example, the solar system has nine planets or nine major planetary bodies orbiting around it. The rate at which an object accelerates as it falls freely on Earth under the influence of gravity is 9.8 meters per second (9.8 m/s^2). The wave theory in physics points to the theoretical possibility of a nine-dimensional universe. The human body is primarily made up of nine major elements, including oxygen, carbon, hydrogen, nitrogen, calcium, phosphorus, potassium, sulfur, and sodium. In meteorology, nine types of cloud formations are used in weather forecasting. Human pregnancy usually lasts for nine months. Geometrically, nine represents a nonagon or a polygon with nine sides. In the Zodiacal signs, the number represents Scorpio. In numerology, the number 9 represents wisdom, introspection, and universal love, resonating with humanitarian values.

In Sanskrit, nine is known as navan, meaning new, similar to Latin novem and Gothic niun, which also means new. The naming suggests that the number nine was regarded in ancient times as a new number, probably because of the practice of counting things in sets of fours using the four fingers, treating four as a limit or break number ². When the four fingers on both hands were used in the counting of something, one had to start with a new set. In Sanskrit, navan is always used as a plural for all three genders. However, its word form may change with each case. When used in a compound word, the last letter, 'n,' is omitted, as in Navaratri (ten days) or Navavidhi (nine ways). In Hinduism, the number nine symbolizes auspiciousness, divinity, diversity, unity, harmony, abundance, diverse manifestations of gods and goddesses, material and spiritual wealth, and pathways to liberation. The following are other important concepts related to the number nine in Hinduism.

- Navami: The ninth day (tithi) of the lunar fortnight in the Hindu calendar is known as Navami. It occurs twice in a lunar month, once in the waxing phase (Shukla Paksha) of the moon and once in the waning phase (Krishna Paksha). Important festivals such as Rama Navami and Durga Navami are celebrated on this day. In Hindu astrology, the day can be auspicious or inauspicious since nine is associated with Mars, which can exert both positive or negative influences and set in motion fiery energies, creating problems and difficulties depending upon the nature of the undertaking, the placement of Mars in a person's birth chart, and other factors.
- Navadravyas: The Vaiseshika philosophy of Hinduism identifies seven primary categories (padarthas) of reality that can be known. One of them is known as Dravyas or substances, which act as the carriers of all the modes (gunas) and actions (karma) of all animate and inanimate things found in creation. They are foundational to the whole existential reality and serve as the basic support or substratum in which all reality and changes manifest. The Vaishesika philosophy identifies nine basic substances or materials (navadravyas), namely earth (Prithvi), water (apa), fire (tejas), air (vayu), ether (akasa), time (kala), direction (dik), self (atman), and mind (manas). They constitute the physical and spiritual "stuff of the universe."
- Navavidha bhakti: The Bhagavata Purana mentions nine forms of devotion meant to establish the mind in divine contemplation and cultivate exclusive devotion, thereby earning God's grace and achieving liberation. They are: Sravanam (hearing

about God), Kirtanam (singing the praise of God), mananam (remembering God), Padaseva (serving the feet of God), Archanam (worshiping God), Mantram (offering prayers to God), Seva (serving the cause of God), Maitri (friendship with God), and Saranam (surrender to God). Devotees may practice one or more of these methods to purify themselves and strengthen their devotion.

- Navagrahas: Hindu astronomy recognizes nine planets, collectively known as Navagrahas. Their movements and configuration are believed to affect the lives, destinies, and planetary influences (grahacharam) of beings in different worlds. The nine planets, or grahas, are the Sun (Surya), the Moon (Chandra), Mars (Mangala), Mercury (Budha), Jupiter (Brihaspati), Venus (Sukra), Saturn (Sani), Rahu, and Ketu. The names of the days in a week are derived from the first seven planets. In Hinduism, the last two grahas are not considered real planets but rather celestial bodies believed to have an evil or negative influence on the moon. However, in Hindu temples, all nine deities are installed together on a single platform, ensuring they do not face each other and are worshipped collectively as a group rather than individually.

- Navadvaras: Hindu scriptures, such as the Bhagavadgita, describe the human body as a city of nine gates (dvaras) because it has nine openings: two eyes, two ears, two nostrils, the navel, and two excretory orifices. It is also likened to a temple with nine entrance doors or gates since the Self resides in the body as its Lord, just as the chief deity in the sanctum of a temple, and interacts with the objective world through them. The organs in the body are likened to the gods in heaven who serve the Self, the Lord of the body. When a person dies, they accompany the Self to the mid-region, where they depart and return to their spheres.

- Navanidhis: Lord Kubera is described as possessing nine treasures which he guards: mahapadma, padma, shankha, makara, kacchapa, mukunda, kunda, nila, and kharva. We find different interpretations of these nine treasures and will not go into detail. These treasures symbolize many auspicious and divine qualities, spiritual and material wealth, as well as peace, prosperity, and abundance. In Hinduism, God is extolled as the giver of these nine treasures (navanidhi ke data).

- Navaratnas: Hindu scriptures refer to nine kinds of jewels or precious stones that are often associated with astrology, mythology, and spirituality, as well as with the nine planets, celestial beings, and divine treasures such as the nine treasures of Kubera mentioned above. The deities in the temples are also adorned with them to denote their opulence. The nine jewels are mukta (pearl), manikya (ruby), vajra (diamond), vaidhurya (cat's eye), gomedhika (hessonite), vidruma (coral), padmaraga (yellow sapphire), marakanta (emerald), and nila (blue sapphire). Each of these nine jewels is associated with a specific planet: pearl with the Moon, ruby with the Sun, diamond with Venus, cat's eye with Ketu, hessonite with Rahu, coral with Mars, yellow sapphire with Jupiter, emerald with Mercury, blue sapphire with Saturn.

- Nava Dhanyas: In Hindu sacrifices and domestic puja ceremonies, nine types of food grains are commonly offered to the gods as a mark of devotion to nourish them and obtain their blessings or fulfill their desires. They symbolize purity, vitality, energy, strength, power, longevity, growth, stability, etc. The nine types of grains are rice (akshata), wheat (godhuma), green gram (moong), bengal gram (chana), black gram (urad), sesame seeds (til), barley (jau or yava), horse gram (kulthi), and finger millet (ragi). They are an integral part of many Hindu ceremonies, especially those aimed at invoking the blessings of divinities for health, wealth, and fertility. They are also used in the installation of idols in temples and the laying of foundations for temples, houses, and other structures, along with the nine kinds of precious stones.

- Nava Durga: The Devi, the Mother Goddess, has numerous forms that represent the energies active in creation and uphold it. Some are described as eight, as in the case of Ashtalakshmi, and some are nine, as in the case of Durga, Chandi, and Kali. In most cases, they align with the nine forms of Shakti or Durga but with different names and functions. The nine Durgas are

Shailaputri, Brahmacharini, Chandraghanta, Kushmanda, Skandamata, Katyayani, Kalaratri, Mahagauri, and Siddhidatri. Each of them represents a unique aspect or energy of the goddess and performs different functions. According to the Puranas, the goddess Durga manifested these forms to slay the demon named Mahishasura. They are also worshipped during the nine days of Navaratri. On this occasion, devotees also worship the nine fierce forms of the goddess Chandi by a special ritual known as Maha Nava Chandi Yagna or Chandipath.
- Nava Rasas: Scriptures such as the Natyashastra outline nine distinct emotions or sentiments (rasas) that are expressed through Indian dance, drama, and literature, which help the performers or the creators connect to their audience. They are shringara (love, beauty, and romance), hasya (laughter and comedy), karuna (compassion and sorrow), raudra (anger and aggression), veera (courage and valor), bhayanaka (fear and horror), bibhatsa (disgust and revulsion, adbhuta (wonder, awe, and amazement, and shanta (peace, composure, and tranquility).
- Nava Ratri: This is a nine-day Hindu festival, also known as Dussehra, during which the goddess Durga and her nine forms are worshipped. Devotees also observe fasting during the nine days, fully or partially.

Reference

1. In Catholic tradition, when a Pope passes away, the Church observes a structured nine-day mourning period called Novemdiales. In Jamaica and other Caribbean nations, relatives hold nine nights of gatherings, prayers, and celebrations before the final burial, a practice that originated from the Asante people of West Africa. Many Catholic communities also observe a nine-day prayer ritual after death, known as a novena.
2. Menninger, Karl. Number Words and Number Symbols. Translated by Paul Broneer. New York: Dover Publications, 1992.

Ten, Dasan

The number ten is the first to emerge from the union of two single digits, one and zero, much like the first word that is manifested in the development of a language from combining two letters. It is an even number and the base of both the decimal and metric systems. It can be divided by 1, 5, and 2 and can be converted into multiples by simply adding zeros. The invention of the decimal system in ancient India revolutionized our understanding of enumeration and computational skills, leading to the exponential growth of our knowledge of the world and the universe. It also helped us control the forces of Nature and establish an advanced civilization. It is a complete number in the sense that it cannot be surpassed without going to the digits below it. It is the foundation of the decimal system (number 10), the most commonly used numeral system in the world, in which the place value increases in powers of ten. It became the norm worldwide after the discovery of zero by Indian mathematicians, vastly improving our understanding of the universe and our ability to solve complex mathematical riddles and theorems, as well as perform intricate logarithms and calculations in science and engineering. Any number that ends in zero is divisible by 10, making it a key factor in simplifying arithmetic. It is also a triangular number since it is the sum of the first four positive integers (1, 2, 3, 4), which can be represented as dots to form a triangle.

Hence, the Pythagoreans revered the number 10 as a "Deity, Heaven, Eternity, and the Sun." They envisioned it as a sacred Tetractys (tetrad), a triangular figure composed of ten points and as the fundamental key to the cosmos, symbolizing the "harmony of opposites," universal order, completeness, divine balance, cosmic structure, eternal life, blueprint of the universe, and "the foundation of music, mathematics, and cosmology." For them, it also represented a "Circle with a visible center" but with a circumference too vast to be seen. They probably drew these based on their belief that the number ten was hidden in various aspects of observable reality, representing celestial harmony and balance, and serving as the key not only to cosmic knowledge and power but also to the mysteries hidden in the cosmos and the numbers that formed its basis. Pythagoras believed in a planetary system consisting of ten celestial bodies: the Sun, the Moon, Mercury, Venus, Mars, Jupiter, Saturn, Earth, the "counter-earth" (a hidden planet opposite Earth), and the heavenly sphere (where the stars were fixed). He also believed in the Music of the Spheres, which postulated that planets and stars emitted vibrations and produced celestial music. Hence, the initiates had to swear to the Tetractys before they were admitted into the school to reinforce the belief that numbers, particularly 10, governed everything from physics to ethics.

Pythagorean teachings influenced several Greek philosophers, including Plato and Aristotle, who believed in the mystical significance of 10 and proposed cosmological theories about souls, rebirth, and the World Soul. Aristotle classified knowledge into 10 categories, called the Ten Categories of Being, which outlined how we understand existence. The Roman numeral for 10 is "X," which also signifies the harmony of the opposites, completeness, balance, order, and perfection. The ancient Egyptians also used a decimal system, probably derived from finger counting. They viewed the number ten as a symbol of perfection and completeness. In Egyptian mythology, their God, Ra, had ten aspects, symbolizing his all-inclusive and encompassing dimensions and the completeness of his vast, supreme powers. In Christianity, the number also has symbolic significance. The Bible mentions the Ten Commandments, the Ten Plagues of Egypt, the Parable of the Ten Virgins, and the healing of ten lepers by Jesus, representing divine order, judgment, completeness, and the importance of ethical conduct.

In Hinduism, the number ten symbolizes wholeness, completeness, dualities, "harmony of the opposites," perfection, all-encompassing reality, mortal life, diversity, unity, totality, balance, symmetry, rebirth, and regeneration. Since it is the first double-digit number formed by the union of one and zero, it stands for creation, the union of Purusha (zero) and Prakriti (1), Isvara, and jiva. The zero stands for Brahman, the pure Self. The number one stands for Brahman's materiality or Prakriti. The number 10, thus, symbolizes Brahman and His manifestation together as one entity, which is well represented by Isvara, the Lord of the Universe, and all the jivas in whom both are also present as one entity. Since the number ten can replicate itself indefinitely and infinitely and reappears in all multiplications, it also represents diversification, reproduction, renewal, regeneration, and creation.

Dasa also indicates power, position, potency, reachability, expansiveness, and might. Things can be grouped into tens or tens of tens. Things can progress or improve tenfold. Ten indicates the diverse aspects of a person, deity, or phenomenon, as in Dasakantha (Ravana), Dasarupabhuta (Vishnu), Dasajit (Rama), or dasaguna (ten virtues). It may describe a person or deity who possesses tenfold strength, power, influence, reach, or control, denoting their superiority, position, strength, or authority. For example, a commander of ten chariots was known as Dasaratha. A head or superintendent of ten villages was called a dashin. Ravana was a mighty king with ten heads (Dashanan), ten necks (Dasakantha), and ten shoulders (Dasakandhara). It meant he possessed tenfold knowledge, power, power of speech, strength, intelligence, and wisdom. These excessive powers and endowments fueled his egoism and delusion and led to his destruction as he used them to oppress others and indulge in evil actions.

The number also represents God's tenfold reach and His active presence in creation. He not only keeps a watch on the whole creation but also incarnates occasionally to restore order and regularity. This is well illustrated by the concept of Dasavataras, or the ten incarnations (Avatars) of Lord Vishnu. According to the Hindu Puranas, he is said to incarnate ten times in this time cycle, of which nine have already occurred, and the tenth incarnation is yet to happen. The number of incarnations alludes to the significance of the number ten as a mystic symbol of God's infinite powers and manifestations and the cyclical nature of His creation. Lord Vishnu is known as Dasarupabhuta since he is the Being (bhuta) with ten forms or incarnations (rupas). Lord Rama is known as Dasaripu, meaning one who killed Ravana, the one with ten heads. His father's name, Dasaratha, means controller and rider of ten chariots. The story of the Ramayana is probably an allegory of God's indomitable might set against an egoistic being who tried to compete with Him with his tenfold powers, strength, and intelligence, and yet ultimately could not match Him. If Ravana was 10, Isvara was 1000. Even with his tenfold powers, he could not prevail because he was just an ordinary Asura who abandoned his divine qualities and spiritual nature and took refuge in his evil nature to take advantage of the boons granted to him by Brahma.

These points illustrate that the number ten has great symbolic significance in Hinduism as God's tenfold physical appearances or divine incarnations in the mortal world. In each incarnation, He physically demonstrates these powers through His actions and glories ten times, a thousand times, or a hundred thousand times, as the situation requires, to revive and reestablish Dharma, destroy evil, and restore people's faith in Him and reinforce the moral imperatives they must follow. Each of His incarnations (avatars) is a conscious and willful union of the transcendental and the immanent, or the eternal and transformative aspects of Brahman. Each time, He manifests fully with tenfold illumination, strength, and resolve in His incarnated body with all His splendor and energies to fulfill the purpose. In a less significant way, but for similar reasons, the number ten symbolizes seers and self-realized yogis who experience oneness with Brahman in their mortal bodies and attain supreme intelligence and illumination. They are different from ordinary mortals because they possess Isvara's divine nature (the 10) and are internally connected to Him through their consciousness.

The extraordinary thing about an incarnation is that the conflict between duality and unity is perfectly resolved into a harmonious whole with no contradictions and no dilution of power and potency, which the incarnation can invoke anytime by exercising His indomitable will. Outwardly, an incarnation may lead an ordinary life and go through the motions of life like any other earthly being. Still, inwardly, He always remains completely conscious of His true nature and the purpose of His incarnation. An incarnation is not an emanation or projection of Isvara but Isvara Himself in a human or mortal form. In the incarnation, He manifests Himself with His full powers. However, in his partial incarnations, manifestations, and emanations, He manifests partially as a divinity, godhead, demi-god, or divine seer. Hence, His incarnations (10s) are a few, while His manifestations (100s, 1000s, 10000s, etc.) are many. Each incarnation appears on Earth for the specific purpose of restoring Dharma, protecting the righteous, and destroying the chaos created by evil entities. Once His task is accomplished, He withdraws from the earth, leaving behind a glorious chapter of His wondrous life, revelations, exemplary conduct, and miraculous actions as an example for posterity to remember and follow in His footsteps.

Apart from these abstract symbolisms, the number ten is associated with many important concepts of Hinduism, such as the following.

- Dasadishas: The concept of dasadishas (ten directions) is rooted in the Rigvedic notion that Brahman is spread in all directions and is omnipresent and omniscient. Hence, in some Vedic rituals, worshippers turn in all directions and offer prayers and invocations. The ten directions are north, south, east, west, northeast, northwest, southeast, southwest, southwest, upward, and downward. Interestingly, the word 'dasa' (ten) is derived from the root word 'das,' and the word 'disa' is derived from the root word 'dis.' The connection between the numerical concept of das and the spatial concept of dis suggests the interconnectedness, completeness, and totality of Brahman and His creation represented in the number ten.
- Dasangulam: The expression ten-fingers wide was often used in the past to refer to the earth or what could be measured by the ten fingers or through the span of ten fingers. For example, the following statement from the Taittiriya Upanishad, "*na bhūmiṁ viśvato vṛtvātyati daśāṅgulam,*" conveys that Brahman is not confined to the physical earth or the material existence by transcends it by ten fingers wide and pervades the whole existence. The expression, ten fingers wide, is used here not only as a unity of measurement but symbolic of spatial expansiveness, which is also suggested by the word dasadisha.
- Dasavidha Dharma: There is no clear description in the scriptures of what constitutes the tenfold Dharma. It may include ten types of virtues, paths of liberation, sacrifices, practices, or duties. One may also use them conveniently according to the occasion, context, or teaching. For example, the five instructions (niyamas) and five restraints (yamas) can be considered the ten

important virtues that are necessary for self-purification. Whatever it may mean, dasavidha dharma refers to a comprehensive set of ten spiritual practices meant for self-purification and liberation, cultivating divine qualities, or upholding Dharma.

- Dasaparamitadhvarah: The Buddha has this as his epithet because of his ten virtues or perfections, which are mentioned in Buddhist texts like the Jataka Tales and the Sutta Pitaka and serve as standing examples for others to follow. They are dana (generosity), sila (morality), nekkhamma (renunciation), panna (wisdom), virya (energy), khanti (patience), sacca (truthfulness), adhitthana (determination), metta (loving-kindness). upekkha (equanimity). Here, the number ten denotes perfection, excellence, or supreme purity.
- Dasapura: It means a city equal to ten cities or formed out of ten cities or villages, symbolizing its vastness, richness, and importance. It is also the ancient name of modern-day Mandsaur in Madhya Pradesh, India, once the capital of a king named Ranti Deva. It got its name because it was ten villages wide, or was created by joining ten villages. According to the inscriptions, such as the Mandsaur pillar inscriptions of the Gupta period (sixth century CE) and the Sanskrit texts, it was a prominent cultural and trade center in ancient times.
- Dasharashmi Shatah: This is an epithet of the Sun, meaning one whose brightness is ten thousand-fold or who has ten thousand rays, symbolizing abundance, vitality, or enlightenment.
- Dasahara: The River Ganga is known as Dasahara because she has the ability to cleanse ten types of sins or impurities and absolve those who take a dip in her waters of their karmic sins. The famous Dussehra festival, which falls on the tenth day of the waxing moon (Shukla Dashami) in the month of Jyeshtha (May–June), is celebrated in honor of Ganga's descent from the heavens to the earth. Dasahara is also an epithet of Durga, who, according to the Puranas, slew ten evil beings. The festival, also known as Dussehra or Vijaya Dashami, is celebrated on the tenth day of the waxing moon in the month of Asvina (September–October) in her honor and in honor of Lord Rama, who

slew the ten-headed Ravana. In both cases, the number ten signifies victory, divinity, power, might, eternity, and invincibility.

Other Numbers

Indians were the first people in history to develop a system of complex enumerations and numerical ladders to count significantly vast numbers and attribute a name to each numerical rank in the system so that one could not only count millions and trillions with ease but also grasp them mentally and visually and use them to measure the dimensions and limits of God's creation. In his book, Number Words and Number Symbols, Karl Menninger writes that among the Indo-European people, Hindus uniquely erected the boldest tower of numbers in existence. "He further adds, *"The Indians have shown a unique gift for abstract numbers. They knew of no better way to honor sacred divinity than counting, which they esteemed far above all merely human endeavors."* Hence, in Hinduism, one can see symbolic significance associated with numbers that are higher than 10. Hindu scriptures mention astronomically large numbers to denote the duration of time cycles or how long life may exist in this world. The numbers, such as 12, 15, 18, 27, 60, 100, 108, and 1000, are considered symbolically significant and are frequently used in general usage as well as in ritual, spiritual, and astrological practices.

Number 11

11 is formed by the union of 1 and 1 and has the same symbolism as that of 2, representing materiality, duality, life, balance, and existence. The human body has 11 organs, including the mind. With hands stretched upward and the body upright, standing on two legs, the body symbolizes 11. The number 11 has significance in the Atharvaveda, which contains 11 Kandas with identical thematic elements and metrical patterns, and with the number of hymns (suktas) equal to the number of the Kanda. The Veda also includes hymns addressed to the 11 Rudras known as the Ekadasha Rudras. The eleventh day of the first and second (white and black) fortnights of the Hindu lunar month is known as Ekadashi, meaning the 11th day of the lunar fortnight, which is considered auspicious in Vaishnavism. On this day, devotees worship Lord Vishnu. Some observe a three-day penance, known as Ekadashi Vratam, fasting fully or partially,

starting from the tenth day (Dashami) and ending on the twelfth day (Dvadashi), as a part of their spiritual practice to control the eleven senses (the ten senses and the mind) and attain self-purification. Ekadashi occurs 24 times a year. Each Ekadashi is known by a specific name and has special significance. Observing penance on this day with self-control and clean thoughts is believed to lead to stability, purity, the grace (anugraha) of Lord Vishnu, and liberation. Followers of Shiva also observe Ekadashi, believing that fasting and worshipping Him on this day pleases Him and leads to purification and liberation.

Number 12

12 symbolizes cosmic harmony, divine order, time, and completeness. 1 symbolizes unity and 2 symbolizes duality, while 12, which results from their union, represents a jiva who contains the Self (1) and experiences duality (2) between himself and others and between his body and his consciousness. Hindu scriptures attest the significance of 12 in creation. The Vedas extol 12 Adityas, solar deities born to Aditi. They represent cosmic order, the movement of the sun during the 12 hours of the day, the progression of time in the 12 months of the year, the 12 divisions of the Cosmos, a Day of Brahma with 12 divisions, which is equal to the cycle of creation, and the 12 spokes in the wheel of Dharma. Several important festivals and events are celebrated on this day in honor of Vishnu and his manifestations and incarnations, such as Kurma, Narasimha, and Vamana. Some believe that Kalki, the tenth incarnation of Lord Vishnu, will manifest on the 12th day of the white lunar fortnight.

Number 13

The number 13, known as Trayodashi in Sanskrit, is a combination of 1 and 3. The number 1 represents Isvara, and the number 3 symbolizes the Trinity: Brahma, Vishnu, and Shiva, as well as His triple functions, namely creation, preservation, and destruction. The 13th lunar day of the Hindu calendar is believed to be sacred by Shiva's ardent devotees. Many observe the fasting penance called Pradosh Vrat for purification and to earn Shiva's grace. Since it is associated with both constructive and destructive forces of creation, the number

13 is regarded by Hindus as both auspicious and inauspicious depending upon the circumstances. Some believe it to be inauspicious due to its astrological association with Rahu and Ketu, planetary deities, who exert an adverse influence on humans born with certain defects in their karmic past and natal charts, especially when other planets are not in their favor. Several Hindus regard it as inauspicious, mainly due to the influence of Western cultures, where the number is feared as a harbinger of misfortune. However, the number has both auspicious and inauspicious qualities. Numerologically, it corresponds to 4, the number that represents stability, balance, harmony, and strength.

Number 14

The number 14 symbolizes transformation, time cycles, karmic balance, and transition from chaos to order and regularity. The number 1 signifies the beginning of transformation or progress, while 4 symbolizes the lunar month, which contains four weeks. The number has significance in numerology as the sum of 1 and 4 is 5, which symbolizes the pyramid. The number 1 represents the top of the pyramid (God and unity), and 4 represents its base. The base with the four sides (square) corresponds to the four-dimensional space or creation. 14 also represents the heaven (1) and the Earth (4), God (1) and His creation (4), a temple sanctum that houses the chief deity with its gopuram and four sides. Thus, 14 represents stability, balance, purity, and harmony. The fourteenth day of each lunar fortnight is called Chaturdashi. In Hindu Tantra, it is considered the time for reflection and spiritual cleansing. Several important festivals fall on this day. The most important ones include Naraka Chaturdashi, Maha Shivaratri, Narasimha Chaturdashi, Ananta Chaturdashi, Vaikuntha Chaturdashi, and Holika. In some parts of India, the day is dedicated to the goddess Kali and observed as Kali Chaudas (meaning the 14th lunar day).

Number 15

Each lunar month of the Hindu calendar is divided into two equal parts (pakshas) of 15 days (tithis), corresponding to the waxing and waning phases of the moon. The waxing or the full moon or the bright half of the month is known as Shukla Paksha, and the waning or the new moon, or the dark half of the month, is known as Krishna Paksha. Each day in each Paksha has its own spiritual and cultural significance, as we have discussed before, and several festivals are celebrated on those days. Thus, the number 15 represents impermanence, mortality, rebirth, recurring cycles of time, our connection to the cosmos and the divinities that regulate and preside over our lives, besides representing light and darkness and other dualities that are inherent to life on Earth. The number is also associated with the Panchadasa mantra of Lalita Tripura Sundari, consisting of 15 syllables, with goddess Lakshmi, who is said to manifest in fifteen forms, and with the 15 tattvas or fundamental realities of Shaivism known as Panchadasa tattvas. Another significant aspect of this day is that both the full moon (Purnima) day and the new moon day (Amavasya) fall on this day. The full moon day is considered auspicious, a day of renewal, life-giving, and spiritually invigorating. Important festivals such as Guru Purnima, Raksha Bandhan, Bauddha Paurnima, etc., fall on this some. Some devotees worship Vishnu or Lakshmi to fulfill their wishes or express devotion. On the new moon day, the sky is pitch dark without the moon. It is considered a time of transition from one fortnight to another and from darkness to light. Some people perform pitru paksha on this day in the month of Bhadrapada (August–September), paying homage to their ancestors, expressing gratitude, seeking blessings, and making offerings to them. Important Hindu festivals like Mahalaya Amavasya and Diwali are celebrated on this day. Both Amavasya and Poornima symbolize the recurring rhythm of the lunar cycle, the transmigration and rebirth of the souls, and the connection between the earth and the moon, between gods and humans, and between the ancestors in the sphere of the moon awaiting their rebirth and their descendants on earth expecting their return, and the continuation of life even after death in the astral plane.

Number 16

The number 16, shodasa, symbolizes divine qualities, the diversity of creation and divine manifestations, and the multiple ways in which we can connect to the deities and worship them. The moon has sixteen phases (shodasa kala). Hence, in the Vedic tradition, people observed fasting for 16 days, incrementally increasing or reducing their food intake for 16 days to cultivate virtues and remove impurities. Hindus celebrate 16 rites of passage (samskaras), starting from the conception and birth of a child and ending with old age and death. Devotees worship the images of gods at homes and in temples by paying homage in 16 ways, which essentially involves making 16 formal offerings with humility and gratitude, such as inviting the deity (avahana), and offering various comforts to the visiting guest: a seat (asana), water for washing feet (padya), water for washing hands (arghya), water for drinking (achamanam), a bath (snanam), clothes (vastra), ornaments (abharana), sandalwood paste (gandha), flowers (pushpa), and so on.

The Prasna Upanishad mentions the sixteen parts or aspects of Purusha, the Cosmic Being, known as Shodasa Kala Purusha, namely prana (life force), shraddha (faith), akasha (space), vayu (air), agni (fire), apas (water), prithvi (earth), indriyas (senses), manas (mind), anna (food), virya (strength), tapas (austerity), mantra (sacred chants) karma (action), lokas (worlds), and nama (name). They denote unity in diversity, the similarities between human and cosmic personalities, and the aspects that govern life on Earth. The number sixteen is also associated with Hindu deities. For example, it is associated with the sixteen phases of (Shodasa kala) Chandra, the moon god, who adorns Shiva's head, and with the 16 aspects of Lalita Tripurasundari, also known as Shodasi, since she is eternally 16 years old with 16 parts and 16 hands that embody her completeness, universality, and association with life, growth, renewal, change, creation, preservation, destruction, and the union of her diverse parts into a harmonious whole. The 16-syllable Shodasi used in the Sri Vidya tradition to invoke her is a powerful mantra. It represents the completeness, beauty, majesty, diversity, and universality of her universal form and the fine integration of her material and spiritual energies. The Nyaya school of philosophy identifies 16 categories (padarthas) that can be identified and conceptualized logically for proper understanding of reality and ourselves. Numerologically, 16 represents 7 (1+6), which is also a sacred number with great significance in Hinduism as described in a previous chapter.

Number 17

Sapatadasi, meaning 10 + 7 in Sanskrit, is not as popular or significant as the numbers 16 or 18, but still carries some religious and spiritual importance. It is a prime number divisible by 1 and itself. Geometrically, it represents a 17-sided polygon. In some cultures, 17 years is considered the threshold age for entering adulthood. It does not hold much symbolic significance in Hinduism, except that some Vedic or Tantric mantras, such as the Chhinnamasta Mantra, may contain 17 syllables, and some prayers may need to be repeated 17 times or in cycles of 17. Numerologically, it combines the power of 1 and 7, both sacred numbers in Hinduism, and represents 8, which stands for stability, infinity, continuity, and balance.

Number 18

For reasons mostly unknown to us, 18 (ashtadasa) has great significance in Hinduism. For example, the Mahabharata has 18 Parvas. The war was fought for 18 days, and a total of 18 divisions (Akshauhinis) on both sides participated in it. The Bhagavadgita, which is a part of the Mahabharata, has 18 chapters. Interestingly, the number of principal Hindu Puranas, which contain stories, genealogies, philosophy, rituals, cosmology, history, and mythology associated with various legendary kings, gods, and goddesses, is 18. Hence, they are known as the Ashtadasa Puranas. The number of secondary Puranas (upapuranas) is also 18. The Shakti Peethas, or the sacred shrines of the Goddess Shakti or the Mother Goddess, representing her universal energy in various forms, are also 18, known as the Ashtadasa Shakti Peethas. These are popular pilgrimage centers, each with a long social, cultural, and religious history and ritual and spiritual distinctions. Each of the 18 goddesses has distinct names, forms, qualities, functions, and potencies, apart from ritual, spiritual, and cultural significance.

Hindu scriptures mention 18 types of study or learning known as Ashatadasa Vidyas. While we do not know clearly what was traditionally included, these 18 subjects are considered very important: the four Vedas, six Vedangas, four Upavedas, and six Darshanas (philosophies) paired into four (Nyaya-Vaiseshika, Samkhya-Yoga,

Mimansa, and Vedanta). In some ancient schools of philosophy or systems of teaching, the list may have varied and could have included the Puranas, Itihasas (epics), Sutras, Tantras, Shastras, or Smritis (law books), and secular subjects such as hunting, fighting, wrestling, arts, crafts, metallurgy, alchemy, etc., in addition to the Vedas, Vedangas and Darshanas. Hindu law books such as the Manusmriti recognize eighteen major causes that lead to disputes (ashtadasa vivadaspadas), namely debt (rina), deposits (nikṣepa), sale without ownership (asvāmivikraya), partnership disputes (sambhūya-samutthāna), non-payment of wages (vetana), breach of contract (samvid-vyatikrama), disputes over property boundaries (simā-vivāda), disputes over land ownership (vastu-vivāda), disputes over inheritance (dāya-vivāda), disputes over gifts (dāna-vivāda), disputes over marriage contracts (vivāha-vivāda), disputes over defamation (abhiyoga), physical assault (danda), theft (steya), robbery and violence (sāhasa), adultery (strī-sangraha), disputes over gambling and betting (dyūta-vivāda), disputes over verbal agreements (vāk-parushya-vivāda).

Numerologically, it represents 9, being a combination of 1 and 8, and is divisible by 2, 3, 6, 9, and itself. When multiplied by any number, the sum of the result is always 9. In Hindu astrology, calculations of planetary movements and their placement are often done in multiples of 18. In Tantric mantras, rituals, and sacred geometry (yantras), 18 is considered a sacred number because of its mystic significance. It is quite likely that the number may have a connection with the universal forms, aspects, and energies of the goddesses and with the methods and means to attain superior knowledge and liberation on the path of liberation. Whatever may be the truth, this recurrence of the number 18 in various forms in Hinduism cannot be a mere coincidence. There must be a hidden symbolism. In some ways, it denotes wholeness, completeness, mastery, holistic wisdom and knowledge, perfection, excellence, the best and highest of something, etc. However, we do not have a clear explanation of what led to its significance, but only speculative theories. The practice of using 18 as a unit of learning, teaching, excellence, etc., may be a remnant of an ancient numeral system or signify the importance of the number nine, which, as we have seen before, symbolizes perfection, completeness, divinity, diversity, harmony, and superiority. It may also have some connection with human life or how a human being comes into existence, since a mother carries her child in her womb for nine months.

Number 108

This is another important sacred number that is used frequently in Hindu rituals and spiritual practices due to its mystical, astronomical, and cosmological significance. Hindus believe that chanting the name of a deity or chanting a mantra or prayer 108 times is auspicious and beneficial. They may also circumambulate a temple or a sacred mound 108 times to cleanse their sins or seek protection from adversity. Uttering 108 names or epithets of deities in domestic worship with devotion is also a standard and popular ritual to propitiate gods. The practice of uttering 108 epithets of a god or goddess is known as Ashtottara Shatanamavali. The epithets used on such occasions reflect the auspicious and distinct qualities, attributes, achievements, powers, and functions of the deity to whom they are addressed. Spiritual people also engage in a similar practice, especially in meditation, during which they recite the names silently, softly, or whisperingly. They use necklaces consisting of 108 beads (japa malas) to keep track of their repetitions. The japa malas are also usually made of either 64 or 108 prayer beads, with one large bead in the middle to facilitate the practice. We do not know clearly why this particular number was chosen in the past for this purpose.

Some suggest that the number signifies the interconnectedness between God and His devotees or between the deities and their worshippers, which can be realized or established through repetitive effort. It may also signify the effort needed by them to please them and fulfill their desires or stabilize their minds in divine contemplation for self-control, peace, and equanimity. The number 108 is also associated with other important concepts. For example, the popular and standard Upanishads are said to be 108. Although this is the traditional belief, there is no unanimity about the Upanishads included in that list. According to the Yoga and Ayurveda traditions, out of 72000 nadis (nerve channels) through which prana flows in the body, 108 nerve channels (nadis) are said to converge at the heart chakra, known as the Anahata Chakra, which is responsible for emotional well-being and positive emotions such as peace, equanimity, compassion, love, and devotion.

It is said that the ratio of the Sun's distance from Earth to its diameter, as well as the Moon's distance from Earth to its diameter, is approximately 108. This may be a coincidence, but considering that Hindus worship the sun and the moon and believe in the existence of an ancestral heaven on the moon and an immortal heaven in the sun, one wonders whether the ancient seers suggested the 108 repetitions in ritual and spiritual practices to attain these worlds. According to some, 108 signifies the cosmic order: 1 symbolizing the universe, 0 representing emptiness, and 8 signifying infinity. From the Hindu perspective, the number signifies the triple entities: Isvara (1), Brahman (0), and Creation (8), which is infinitely and repetitively cyclical, with Brahman as the common and uniting aspect of both. The practice of repeating mantras or names, ringing the bells in temples, or rotating the prayer wheels 108 times for cleansing one's karma or pleasing the gods is also followed in Buddhist meditation and ritual worship.

Number 116

This number does not carry as much importance as 108 in Hindu ritual or spiritual practices. It comes up mostly in the gifting customs of the Telugu people of Andhra Pradesh and Telangana, where it is common to give cash gifts of ₹116 or ₹1116 on important occasions such as marriages, birthdays, anniversaries, making temple donations, etc. Although no religious or spiritual significance is attached to it, the practice began a few centuries ago when India was still under British rule and parts of Andhra Pradesh and Telangana were under Nizam rule. Two currencies circulated in these regions: the British anna system and the Nizam system. When they had to follow the British system, people in the Nizam territory paid extra to account for the difference between the two currencies. This is how the tradition of giving ₹116 or ₹1116 started in these areas. The 16 rupees compensated for the difference in the values of the two currencies for every 100. The practice persisted even after the Nizam rule ended, and the territories under his rule became part of independent India. Even now, people consider it auspicious (shagun) to give cash gifts in this manner. A similar practice prevails in Tamil Nadu and parts of Northern India, where cash gifts are given in sums that end with 1, such as ₹101, ₹501, or ₹1001, etc., instead of round numbers due to the same belief that it is auspicious and beneficial.

Astronomical numbers

From an early history, Indians developed a system of counting large numbers, some too large even to conceive. One hundred was Shata, 10^2. Sahasra was 10^3. Ayuta was 10^4. Niyuta or Laksha was 10^5, and Prayuta, a million, was 10^6. There were even higher numbers: a Koti (10^7), Ayuta (10^9), Niyuta (10^{11}), Vivara (10^{15}), Bahula (10^{23}), and so on, all the way up to Vibhutangama (10^{51}) and Tallakshana (10^{53}). According to Karl Menninger [1], the importance of such large number ladders "lies not in any clear conception of numbers (for who can visualize a number like 10^{53}?) but in their underlying recognition that a tower can be built up, level upon level, and that the tower of numbers rises high above the world of mortals to realm of gods and 'Enlightened.' For us, however, their greatest significance is the fact that their gradations clearly build up to invisible superhuman heights, like the successive levels of an Indian temple; and - most important of all – the ranks are named"

Time (Kala) has great significance in Hinduism. It is considered one of the highest manifestations of Brahman. It is also associated with Death and represents Death (Kala) since, in the mortal world, everyone must depart when their time is due. In Hinduism, Death is considered the lord of the mortal or the material world, since everything here is subject to impermanence, death, decay, and destruction. However, even the finite world of God's creation is large, with unfathomable dimensions. As modern science reveals, a small galaxy in the universe is too vast for the human mind to conceive. Indeed, in the Bhagavadgita, Lord Krishna shows the universal form of Death, known as Mahakala, to Arjuna to let him know how vast His creation is, and how no one can escape from the fate He ordains to happen and the fiery jaws of Death. In Hinduism, Time is conceived as one of Brahman's highest manifestations and is measured differently in different worlds. For example, a year of human time is equal today in the world of Indra. Hence, on a cosmic scale, it is measured in small as well as in large units.

The small units of time are stated below. They show the precision with which the ancient astrologers of India conceptualized and measured time in the smallest units possible that are beyond human comprehension.

- Paramāṇu: The smallest unit, or a fraction of a second, which is about 16.8 microseconds.
- Anu: Equal to two Paramāṇu, approximately 33.7 microseconds.
- Truti: Equal to 3 Anu, about 1/3290th of a second.

Large units of time

Apart from the above, ancient Indians used large units of time to measure days, weeks, months, and years. The Surya Siddhanta, Manusmriti, Bhagavata Purana, and Vishnu Purana are some of the key sources that outline these divisions.

- Nimesha: Roughly equal to the time taken for the blink of an eye, or 0.213 seconds.
- Kshana: Equal to three Nimesha or about 0.64 seconds.
- Muhurta: Equal to 48 minutes, often used to set the time for rituals and auspicious beginnings or undertakings. They are further divided into auspicious and inauspicious periods.
- Ahorātra: A full day (dina) and night divided into 30 Muhurtas.
- Tithi: Begins at sunrise and ends when the Moon completes a shift of 12 degrees in its angular distance from the Sun.
- Vara: Equal to seven days
- Paksha: Equal to 15 tithis (days) of the lunar fortnight. Each lunar month comprises two pakshas: Shukla Paksha, the waxing phase of the Moon (from New Moon to Full Moon), and Krishna Paksha, the waning phase of the Moon (from Full Moon to New Moon). Depending upon the Tithi, Vara, Nakshatra, and the placement of planets, they can be auspicious or inauspicious.
- Masa: A lunar month equal to 30 tithis.

Extremely large units of time

The Vedic scriptures and Vedic cosmology refer to the following astronomical units of time to signify the immeasurability of God's creation.

- Brahma's life span: 100 Brahma years. Each full day of Brahma (day and night) is equal to roughly 8.64 billion human years. His full lifespan is about 311 trillion and 40 billion Earth years.
- Kalpa: A day (12 hours from morning to evening) in the life of Brahma is known as Kalpa. It is equal to the duration of a cycle of creation from the beginning to the end and is said to last for 4.32 billion Earth years. In the other half of the day (night), he rests for the same period.
- Manvantara: Each reign of a Manu, the progenitor of human races, is known as Manvantara, which lasts for 306,720,000 years. In each Kalpa, 14 Manus reign. Each of them has a specific name, distinguishing qualities, roles, and functions.
- Sandhya: The intervening period of rest between a preceding and a following Manvantara is known as Sandhya (Twilight). It lasts for 1,728,000.
- Mahayuga: A great epoch or vast period that lasts about 4,320,000 years. Each Manvantara is divided into 71 Mahayugas.
- Yugas: Each Mahayuga is further divided into four epochs or yugas, namely Krita (Satya), Treta, Dvapara, and Kali Yugas, with a duration of 1,728,000 years, 1,296,000 years, 864,000 years, and 432,000 years, respectively. According to Hindu astronomical calculations, we are currently in Kaliyuga. However, we do not know exactly when it started. According to the Mahabharata and other scriptures, it began with the conclusion of Lord Krishna's incarnation on Earth.

Reference

1. Menninger, Karl. Number Words and Number Symbols. Translated by Paul Broneer. New York: Dover Publications, 1992.

Numbers in Hindu Philosophy

It is interesting to note that Hinduism has a school of philosophy based on numbers known as the philosophy of numbers (Sankhya). The school describes the number of primary realities (tattvas) of creation and how they produce diversity through aggregation. Indeed, in Hinduism, philosophy itself is called tattva jnana or the science of tattvas because it essentially deals with the nature of reality or realities. The Yoga philosophy, which is closely aligned with the number system of Samkhya, has the number eight as its thematic symbol. The system it proposes is known as the Eightfold Yoga (Ashtanga Yoga). Some schools believe that the number of souls in creation is infinite, while some believe that they are predetermined and fixed. Numbers are, thus, at the heart of Hindu philosophical thought.

One of the defining aspects of Advaita (nondualism) is the number one. It believes that Brahman, the absolute, supreme reality, is one and only, and the rest is an illusion. On the other hand, Dvaita (dualism) has the number two as its principal theme, as it upholds the dualities found in creation between God and souls, souls and souls, as permanent and eternal. The Vishistadvaita philosophy identifies three types of souls: the eternally free souls, the liberated souls, and the bound souls. The Tantra tradition of Hinduism is even more number-oriented as the mystic diagrams used in rituals and contemplative practices contain many numbers depicted in them as the essential aspects of Prakriti or Shakti.

The Hindu philosophy is traditionally divided into six schools known as Darshanas. Each refers to a viewpoint, perspective, or vision, each with a long history and further subdivisions. They contain several concepts, categories, or groups that are associated with numbers. We have already discussed some of them in the previous chapters in reference to the specific numbers with which they are associated. For readers' convenience, we are stating them again briefly.

24-36 Tattvas or divisions

Tattvas are the primordial aspects, divisions, or principles of Nature

(Prakriti) that manifest in creation as bodily organs or parts, performing specific functions and imparting distinct forms and identities to living beings. The Samkhya School identifies 24 tattvas: Prakriti, Mahat (intelligence), Ahankara (ego), Manas (mind), 5 Jnanedriyas (organs of perception), 5 Karmendriyas (organs of action), 5 Tanmatras (subtle essences), 5 Mahabhutas (elements). These tattvas manifest in existence in the same order from Prakriti. Of these, Prakriti is productive only, meaning that it produces other tattvas. Mahat, Ahamkara, and Tanmatras are both productions and productive (meaning they arise from other tattvas and produce further tattvas), while the remaining ones are only productions. Shaivism identifies 36 tattvas: 5 Isvara tattvas (Shiva, Shakti, Sadashiva, Isvara, Suddha Vidya), 5 Shakti Tattvas (Kala, Niyati, Vidya, Raga, Kala), 6 Atma Tattvas (Maya, Purusha, Buddhi, Ahamkara, Manas, and Prakriti), 5 Jnanendriyas (organs of perception), 5 Karmendriyas (organs of action), 5 Tanmatras, and 5 Mahabhutas. Spiritual practice in Hinduism is meant to cleanse these tattvas so that they shine fully with the light of the Self without obstructions.

16 Padarthas or Categories

The concept of Padarthas is peculiar to Nyana and Vaiseshika schools. A Padartha is a Category of reality that is either physical or mental, gross or subtle, and can be definitively known, recognized, and named due to its peculiarity, quality, or condition. Pada means word, and artha means meaning. A Padartha is a word-meaning that can be attributed or associated with any objectified, distinguishable, and unique aspect of existential reality. The Nyaya School recognizes 16 categories (padarthas) of experiential and objective reality. Since the school primarily emphasizes logic and epistemology, these categories are primarily related to logical thinking and reasoning that are necessary to cultivate the right knowledge and discernment. The categories are 1. Pramana (means of valid knowledge), 2. Prameya (objects of valid knowledge), 3. Samsaya (doubt), 4. Prayojana (purpose, utility), 5. Dṛṣṭanta (precedent, example, instance), 6. Siddhanta (established theory, rule, or conclusion), 7. Avayava (parts of syllogism), 8. Tarka (philosophical, hypothetical, or speculative reasoning), 9. Nirṇaya (final judgment, determination, settlement, decision), 10.

Vada (argument or discussion), 11. Jalpa (quarrelsome wrangling or disputation), 12. Vitanda (unreasonable argument), 13. Hetvabhasa (fallacious argument), 14. Chala (deceitful or evasive argument), 15. Jati (intelligent refutation with clever arguments), and 16. Nigrahasthana (a position from where it is difficult to continue an argument or discussion).

The Vaishesika School, which is traditionally paired with the Nyaya philosophy, identifies seven Padarthas or Categories instead of the latter's 16. They are Dravya (nine primary substances with qualities and activity that constitute the materiality of the whole existence from which all things arise), Guna (24 generic and specific qualities associated with the substances mentioned before), Karma (five actions or movements associated with the substances that are peculiar or common to them), Samanya or Jati (generic features common to a class of substances), Vishesa (particular features that distinguish each substance from others of the same class), Samvaya (inherence or the intimate and inseparable relationship between entities in which at least one is necessary for the other to exist, like parts cannot exist without the whole), and Abhava (nonexistence of things or substances which may arise in four situations).

Nine Dravyas or substances

The Vaiseshika philosophy holds that all products or objects arise from elementary substances called Dravyas. These substances form the basis of the material universe and act as the substrate for the qualities and activities that manifest in objects and distinguish them. According to this school, the substances are nine: earth (prithvi), water (ap), fire (tejas), air (vayu), ether (akasa), time (kala), space (dik), Self (Atman), and mind (manas). The first four are the elements (bhutas), created by the aggregation of atoms (paramanus) that are eternal, indivisible, and indestructible. Gross objects, such as pots, are made up of them. The fifth element, ether, is devoid of atoms. Space is not empty but filled with ether. Both time and ether are infinite. The Self is eternal and all-pervading. It has attributes in the bound state, but is free from them in the state of liberation. The mind is an instrument, is specific to each Self or jiva and does not produce any material things, unlike the first four substances.

Six Darshanas or philosophies

Hinduism has six schools of philosophy known as Darshana, which means a vision, perspective, or point of view. The six schools are Nyaya, Vaiseshika, Samkhya, Yoga, Purva Mimansa, and Uttara Mimansa. The last one is also known as Vedanta. They are grouped into three pairs: Nyaya and Vaishesika, Samkhya and Yoga, and Purva and Uttara Mimansa because of their identical beliefs and doctrinal matters. All six schools belong to the traditional Astika system, which believes in the existence of God and the afterlife, and the supremacy and authority of the Vedas. Hinduism also had several Nastika schools, which did not believe in the existence of God.

Pramanas or methods of validation

The methods, sources, or means by which proofs are validated and truths are established are known as pramanas. They help us ascertain valid knowledge, draw the right conclusions, or arrive at the right understanding, agreement, or judgment. Purva Mimansa School acknowledges six Pramanas: perception (pratyaksha), inference from available facts (anumana), comparison (upamana), verbal testimony (sabda), drawing presumptions based on common features (arthapatti), and ascertaining the nonexistence of something through noncognition (anupalabdhi). The school considers verbal testimony or expert opinion drawn from authoritative texts, such as the Vedas, as the supreme source of validation. The Nyaya school acknowledges four pramanas: perception, inference, comparison, and testimony. The Vaishesikas accept only two: perception and inference. The remaining schools accept three of them: perception, inference, and testimony.

Five Yamas and Niyamas

The yamas are the restraints or what one should refrain from doing on the path of liberation for self-purification. The Yoga school identifies five yamas: ahimsa (nonviolence), satya (truthfulness), asteya (no-stealing), brahmacharya (restraining the sexual impulse), and aparigraha (no-coveting). Of them, the commentators of the Yogasutras acknowledge nonviolence as the most important since all other virtues lead to it. The school also prescribes five ethical rules or observations called niyamas to inculcate discipline and self-control: saucha (cleanliness), santosha (contentment or positivity), tapa (austerity), svadhyaya (self-study), and Isvara-pranidhana (devotion to the God who resides in the body).

Seven bhumis or stages of consciousness

The Yogasutras of Patanjali mentions (2.27) seven stages of discriminative intelligence or insightful awareness (viveka-khyati) arising from self-absorption (samadhi) when ignorance is completely removed and the conjunction between the Self and the gunas is fully resolved. There is no unanimity among the scholars and yoga gurus about these seven stages. According to some, they refer to the different stages of awareness that arise from the same state of self-absorption. According to some, they refer to different degrees of insightful awareness or discernment that arise sequentially prior to self-realization when even buddhi becomes detached from Purusha (the Self), falls silent, and one remains fully established in the Self with no other awareness.

Five Chittavrittis or mental modifications

In the Yogasutras, Patanjali describes five kinds of chittavrittis, meaning mental whirls, modifications, disturbances, or changing states of the mind. The five types of modifications that keep the mind disturbed and unstable are: right knowledge, wrong knowledge, imagination, sleep, and memory. The first one arises from the three pramanas: perception, inference, and verbal testimony, or the study of the scriptures. The second type of modification, false knowledge, arises from faulty perception or misapprehension due to carelessness, ignorance, or delusion. In imagination, the mind creates knowledge on its own, without corresponding objective reality, which cannot be construed as right or wrong knowledge arising from perception, inference, or testimony. Deep sleep is a mental modification (chitta vrittis) because it induces tamas and suppresses rajas and sattva, in which objects do not shine in the consciousness, and one is fully absorbed in ignorance. In memory, the mind hangs on to the objects arising from perception, inference, and testimony, and those images keep the mind disturbed. In the Yogasutras, Patanjali states that the purpose of Yoga is to suppress these modifications and still the mind so that the Purusha remains free from them and abides in His own consciousness.

2-8 Angas or limbs of yoga

The Classical Yoga System of Patanjali consists of eight distinct methods, techniques, or practices known as angas. Hence, it is also called Ashtanga Yoga or the Eightfold Yoga. The eight limbs are yama (restraints), niyama (observances), asana (postures), pranayama (breathing practices), pratyahara (withdrawal of the mind and senses), dharana (concentration), dhyana (meditation), and samadhi (stilling the mind). These practices eventually lead to the detachment of Purusha (the Self) from the mind and body, whereby it remains established in its own nature, which is characterized by truth, bliss, and pure consciousness. The Tantra tradition of Hinduism, and texts such as the Maitri Upanishad (6.18), mention a six-limbed yoga known as Shashtanga Yoga, consisting of six distinct practices, namely pratyahara, dharana, dhyana, samadhi, tarka (philosophical inquiry), and suddhi (self-purification). Some Hindu texts also mention twofold, threefold, and fivefold yogas.

Three Types of Karmas or Duties

The Mimansa schools identify different types of karmas (sacrifices). They divide the sacrifices mainly into two categories: obligatory and optional. The former constitute obligatory duties (dharma), and the latter are known as kamya karma (desire-ridden actions). According to the Vedas, one may perform obligatory duties to fulfill desires, but it is not recommended since it leads to sin and suffering. Tradition discourages kamya karmas since they invariably lead to bondage and suffering. Obligatory duties are further divided into daily sacrifices (nitya karma) and occasional sacrifices (naimittika karma). Those who take up householder duties must perform them as prescribed by the Vedas to avoid sinful consequences, rebirth, and bondage to samsara, since they are essential for life on Earth and arise primarily from the duties God Himself performs for the order and regularity of the worlds. Daily sacrifices such as nourishing gods, ancestors, seers, sages, and other beings must be performed every day.

Occasional sacrifices must be performed according to the Hindu calendar on auspicious occasions or to celebrate important events in the lives of humans. Apart from these, the Vedas prohibit the faithful from indulging in certain actions. They are called nishiddha karmas and must be avoided by all means as they can lead to mortal sins and grave consequences.

Five Virtues, five sins, and six vices

Hindu texts such as the Bhagavadgita and the Dharma Shastras identify several virtues. Of them, five are considered cardinal virtues: purity, self-control, detachment, truthfulness, and nonviolence [2]. Hindu law books such as the Manusmriti and other Dharma Shastras declare five actions produce the gravest sin. They should be avoided by all: 1. brahmahatya (killing a Brahmana dedicated to Dharma), 2. surapana (consuming alcohol and other intoxicating substances), 3. Steya (stealing from others), 4. gurvanganagama (illicit relation with a teacher's wife), and 5. samsarga (association with those who commit these sins). Hindu law books also identify six chief evil passions or enemies of the mind known as arishadvargas or shadripus, namely kama (lust), krodha (anger), lobha (greed), moha (delusion, infatuation, or attachment), mada (egoistic pride), and matsarya (envy). Manu states that those who succumb to these passions fall into darkness. According to the Bhagavadgita, one must overcome them by conquering the gunas to achieve liberation.

Four types of karma

Karma means both actions, as well as the results or consequences of those actions. By this definition, all the obligatory duties that constitute one's Dharma and all the sacrifices, rites, and rituals prescribed by the Vedas and the tradition also fall under the definition of karma. The karma that arises from a jiva's actions influences that jiva's destiny and future lives. Since this karma is directly linked to one's actions (karma), one must live responsibly to avoid sinful karma. However, it is not the best solution. According to the Bhagavadgita, one must resolve all karma by offering all actions to God along with their results. Hinduism recognizes four types of karma that arise from our actions and simultaneously influence our lives and births: Sanchita

Karma, Prarabdha Karma, Agami Karma, and Kriyamana Karma. Sanchita Karma represents all the karma that accumulates from one's previous lives. It is the burden of your past that has been deposited in your account and must be exhausted at some stage through your actions for your liberation. Prarabdha Karma is the portion of your Sanchita Karma that is currently active and influences your present life and circumstances. Depending upon the nature of your actions, you are either exhausting it or creating more karma for yourself. Agami Karma arises from your current actions and is added to your Sanchita Karma, whose consequences you will experience in your future births. Kriyamana Karma is the karma that bears fruit either now or in the future, but in any case, in this very birth.

Panchikarana, Fivefold mixing of elements

Hindu texts such as Atmabodha, Tattvabodha, and the Paingala Upanishad describe how Isvara, the Lord of the Universe, manifests the five gross elements (space, air, fire, water, and earth) from the five subtle elements (tanmatras: sound, touch, form, taste, and smell) through a process of mixing known as panchikarana. According to these texts, Isvara, the Lord of the Universe, divided each of the five subtle elements into two equal parts. He kept one part intact while dividing the other into four equal parts again. Then, He combined the four parts of each subtle element with the four halves of the remaining four subtle elements to produce five gross elements. As a result, each gross element contains half of the corresponding subtle element and one-eighth of each of the remaining four gross elements. The Paingala Upanishad [3] states, "From these, he created endless crores of macrocosms, fourteen worlds specific to (each of these macrocosms) and globular gross bodies fit for each (of these worlds). " These fivefold mixtures of subtle elements were further mixed in various permutations and combinations with the triple modes (sattva, rajas, and tamas), to manifest all the diversity in creation. As per Shankara, forms that manifest from this fivefold mixing are subject to six modifications: existence, birth, growth, change, decay, and death. The process also symbolizes the harmony and interconnectedness of creation, the transformation of subtle energies of the universe into gross energies and forms, the threefold and fivefold aspects of

Sacred Number of Hinduism

creation, and the sacred geometry found in the mystic diagrams and formulae of Hindu Tantra, such as the pentagon, the multilayered structure of Sri Yantra, and the relationship and similarity between the macrocosm of God and the microcosm of the jivas.

Reference

1. tathā tat prayoga-kalpaḥ—prāṇāyāmaḥ pratyāhāro dhyānaṁ dhāraṇā tarko samādhiriti ṣaḍaṅgāni
2. Mahadevan, T. M. P. Outlines of Hinduism. Mumbai: Chetana Limited, 1960.
3. Jayaram, V. 2013. Paingala Upanishad. In Selected Upanishads, translated by Jayaram V. New Albany, OH: Pure Life Vision LLC.

Epilogue

We have seen how numbers play an important role in Hinduism as manifestations of divinities and energies of the mind, body, and the universe, and serve the same purposes as the deities, idols, and mantras of the sacred realms. They reveal to us the hidden patterns of creation and the secrets that are hidden in the universal intelligence (Mahat) that creates all this. Under a guru's guidance, numbers can help us practice concentration and meditation and realize the divinities hidden in them or preside over them and the phenomena they represent. The presiding deity of zero is Brahman, of one is Isvara, of two is Prakriti or the Goddess, of three is the Trinity, and so forth. As someone said, the fractions represent the infinities hidden within infinities and the realities hidden within realities. The material world we experience through the senses is a construction designed by God based on numbers and number patterns, formulas, or equations. They are the footprints that the divine has left in the layers of His manifestations for us to meditate on and realize their significance. They are the stepping stones to higher awareness and self-realization. We have the choice to contemplate and marvel at God's creation, discern the secrets hidden in them, and withdraw into zero, the absolute reality, or extend our minds and intelligence into the superficial aspects of our existence, becoming attached to relative truths, dualities, and diversity, and remaining bound.

Cover Design by Jayaram V

www.ingramcontent.com/pod-product-compliance
Lightning Source LLC
Chambersburg PA
CBHW061808070526
44586CB00024B/2763